STEPPING BEYOND YOUR COMFORT ZONE
UNLEASHING YOUR INNER GREATNESS

DR. VALARIE W. HARRIS

STEPPING OUT
WITH PURPOSE

Stepping Beyond Your Comfort Zone

Copyright © 2024 Dr. Valarie W. Harris

Published by
Stepping Out with Purpose
steppingout@talktimeval.com

Anthology Editor
Chandra Sparks Splond, M.S.E.
www.chandrasparkssplond.com

ISBN: 979-8-9877190-4-6. (Paperback)
ISBN: 979-8-9877190-5-3. (Hardback)

Book Design by Brand It Beautifully™ at www.branditbeautifully.com

This book is dedicated to you, Dear Reader, for your courage, resilience, and unwavering spirit.

Within you lies an untapped reservoir of strength, capable of overcoming any challenge, obstacle, or setback.

May these pages' stories, principles, and strategies elevate your spirit, enlighten your mind, and empower your heart. Let them remind you that the greatness inside of you is a light that the world needs, especially in times of darkness. You are capable of more than you ever imagined, and it's time to unleash that potential.

Here's to stepping beyond your comfort zone and into the extraordinary life you were meant to live.

CONTENTS

INTRODUCTION

In the pages of *Stepping Beyond Your Comfort Zone,* you'll embark on a transformative journey guided by the wisdom and expertise of seven enthusiastic women. This collaborative effort brings together the essence of personal empowerment, inspiring stories, and actionable advice to lead you on a path of growth and change.

As you delve into the contents of this book, you'll find that our approach is infused with positivity and a transferrable energy that will draw you in and set the tone for your own journey of self-discovery. With a firm belief in the greatness that resides within each of us, we offer concrete, achievable steps that empower you to take charge of your personal development.

That's not all.

In this collaborative effort, the insights and experiences of these remarkable women leaders exemplify excellence in their respective fields. These women have made a significant impact on a large scale, and their expertise spans a diverse spectrum—from education and business to humanitarian causes and beyond. Their stories serve as beacons of inspiration and testimony to the incredible heights that can be reached when one steps beyond their comfort zone.

The heart of our content lies in empowering statements, and we'll frame our guidance within frameworks and principles that give structure to your growth journey. We'll challenge you with thought-provoking questions that invite you to reflect on your situation and ambitions.

Throughout this book, you'll also encounter relatable stories, insightful guidance, authentic life experiences, and challenges that add depth and wisdom to our advice. Storytelling is a powerful tool we employ to illustrate concepts and drive home the importance of stepping out of your comfort zone.

Stepping Beyond Your Comfort Zone is more than a book; it's a beacon of inspiration and a roadmap for personal transformation. Get ready to embrace growth and change like never before as you join us on this empowering journey, accompanied by the wisdom of these amazing women leaders whose excellence knows no bounds.

WALKING IN PURPOSE
DR. TERESA A. BENNETT

In the realm of personal growth and development exists a powerful concept that holds the key to unlocking our true potential. It is a concept that many of us are familiar with, yet often struggle to embrace fully. This concept is just stepping out of our comfort zone and walking in purpose.

Our comfort zone is a familiar and cozy place. It is where we feel safe, secure, and in control. Within its confines, we are shielded from the uncertainties and challenges that lie beyond. But while our comfort zone provides us with a sense of stability, it also limits our growth and hinders our ability to reach new heights.

Stepping out of our comfort zone is a challenging feat. It requires us to confront our fears, face uncertainty, and embrace discomfort. It demands that we push past our self-imposed boundaries and venture into uncharted territory. It calls for courage, resilience, and a willingness to embrace change.

Stepping out of my comfort zone to walk in purpose was daunting, but doing so led to personal and professional growth. In my case, pursuing a doctorate degree was an incredible journey that required me to push myself beyond my limits and embrace challenges. Here is how I successfully stepped out of my comfort zone, conquered my fears, and obtained my well-deserved doctorate degree.

CONQUERING MY FEARS

Stepping out beyond my comfort zone was one of the most transformative experiences of my life. However, it was a journey filled with uncertainty, doubt, fear, immense growth, self-discovery, and achievement.

Fear is a natural emotion that has been hardwired into our very being. It is an instinctual response designed to protect us from harm. However, fear can also hinder our progress, hold us back, and prevent us from reaching our full potential. It becomes a barrier that keeps us confined within the limits of our comfort zone, which is that place where familiarity and predictability reign supreme. It is a space where we feel safe and secure, shielded from the unknown.

Stepping out of my comfort zone meant venturing into uncharted territory, where uncertainty and discomfort would become my constant companions. It required me to confront my deepest fears head-on.

The first step in overcoming my fears was to acknowledge that fear existed. We all have fears, big or small, rational or irrational. Our fears can range from the fear of failure, rejection, or public speaking to the fear of the unknown, change, or even success. Whatever the fear, it is essential to recognize it and admit its influence over our lives. More importantly, it is vital to remember that we serve a great God who can do exceedingly above all that we could ever imagine. I had to remind myself, *"Greater is he that is in me than he that is in the world"* (1 John 4:4.).

Once I identified areas of fear in my life, the next step was understanding their origins. Anxiety often stems from past experiences, beliefs, or traumas that have left an indelible mark on our psyche. By delving into the root causes of my fears, I gained valuable insight into why they held such power over me. This self-awareness opened the door to healing and growth.

Conquering my fears required a courageous mindset and a willingness to overcome discomfort. It was about embracing the unknown, vulnerability, and the possibility of failure. It was about redefining my relationship with fear and reframing it as a growth and personal development catalyst. Taking a small step outside of my comfort zone was incredibly empowering. Each small step built momentum and strengthened my resilience, making it easier for me to face more significant fears that I would face in the future.

Surrounding myself with a supportive network was crucial when facing my fears. Having cheerleaders like my loving daughter and sister, my mentors, and accountability partners provided the encouragement and motivation I needed to push through the inevitable challenges I would face. They reminded me of my strengths, offered guidance, and celebrated my victories.

Remember, our fears do not define us. They are merely temporary obstacles that can be overcome with determination, perseverance, and self-belief. By stepping out beyond our comfort zone and facing our fears head-on, we unlock a world of untapped potential and discover the true extent of our capabilities. In the end, facing our fears is not about eliminating fear entirely but learning to navigate it and harness its power. It is about embracing discomfort, seeking growth, and the limitless possibilities that lie outside the confines of our comfort zone. With that in mind, I was encouraged to take that first step, which began a journey filled with courage, resilience, and incredible personal growth.

FINDING MY MOTIVATION

Stepping out of my comfort zone meant venturing into uncharted territory where uncertainty and discomfort would become my constant companions. It required me to confront my deepest fears head-on. As I began the process of pursuing my doctorate degree, I was faced with a mountain of fear. Was I smart enough? Can I work a full-time job and pursue a terminal degree? Can I afford this fourth degree? These were just some fears that held me hostage as I began my doctoral journey.

I was motivated to step out of my comfort zone, first because getting a doctoral degree was part of God's plan and purpose for my life; additionally, I knew that pursuing a terminal degree would provide an opportunity for me to acquire the knowledge and skills that I needed to move to the next level in my professional career. Further, obtaining a doctorate degree would show my younger family members (nieces and nephews) that they could obtain an advanced degree if they were willing to put in the hard work.

I was motivated by my ancestors on whose shoulders I stood. My ancestors made many sacrifices that enabled me to pursue a doctoral degree. Many of our ancestors were not able to obtain a formal education, but they paved the way for me to attend colleges and universities to which I might not otherwise have access. I was motivated by the love and sacrifices of my parents. I wanted to make them proud of my accomplishments.

I was motivated to challenge myself to embrace new experiences. It was important to me to branch out rather than remain complacent, as I had done so much in the past. It is important for me to share at this point that finding motivation was not a one-time event but an ongoing process that I had to revisit several times during my doctoral journey. It required me to set long-term goals, which aided in me breaking free of the limitations I had placed upon myself and daring myself to do something big. I took on tasks and projects that excited and scared me simultaneously. I remember the moment I decided to submit my application to the doctoral program; it was exciting but oh so scary at the same time. At that moment, I decided I would not let fear stop me, but I would step out of my comfort zone and allow courage to guide me. I had to be patient and kind to myself. I knew there could be setbacks and failures along the way, but instead of viewing them as roadblocks, I saw them as opportunities to learn, adjust, and keep moving forward. Finding my motivation required a willingness to step into the unknown, embrace discomfort, and challenge myself to grow. These experiences uncovered my true passion and ignited the fire within.

DEVELOPING MY GOALS

One powerful tool that assisted me on my doctoral journey was developing goals. My goals were a beacon of light that guided me toward my ultimate prize. My goals gave me direction and purpose and pushed me to stretch beyond what I thought was possible. As I set goals to obtain my degree, I visualized the outcome I desired to achieve. My goals helped to paint a vivid picture of what success would look like for me. The clarity fueled my motivation and determination, pushing me to take the necessary steps to turn my dreams into reality. How did I go about developing my goals? It began with self-reflection and introspection. I took time to truly understand my values, passions, and aspirations. Gaining a deep understanding of who I am and what I want allowed me to align my goals with my authentic self. After clarifying my desires, it was time to set SMART (specific, measurable, achievable, relevant, and time-bound) goals. My SMART goals allowed me to create a roadmap toward my doctoral degree. This was an ongoing process; therefore, I needed to revisit and revise my goals often to ensure they aligned with my purpose.

TAKING ACTION

We can dream, plan, and visualize all we want, but only through taking action can we truly transform our lives. Taking action is pivotal when bridging the gap between our aspirations and reality. It is when we no longer settle for our comfort zone's familiar, safe confines. It is the moment when we choose to push ourselves beyond the boundaries we have set for ourselves.

Taking action to commit to the doctoral journey was like declaring to myself and the universe that I was committed to achieving my dreams. But it took work. It required me to confront my fears, face uncertainty, and embrace discomfort. It demanded that I step into the unknown, leaving behind the safety net of familiarity. But it was precisely at this moment that I realized my strength and resilience.

Taking action for me was about more than just big, grand gestures. It was about the small steps I had to take daily toward my goal. It was in the small details, like reading articles in my subject area, writing daily, and building my network. When I began to take action, the journey started for me.

DEALING WITH SETBACKS

As I took bold steps and embraced new challenges toward my purpose, setbacks inevitably became a part of my path. These setbacks tested my resilience and determination, forcing me to confront the discomfort and uncertainty that comes with venturing into uncharted territory. In the face of setbacks, it was only natural to feel discouraged. I was even tempted to retreat into the familiarity of my comfort zones. However, it was through adversity that I developed resilience, strength, and the unwavering belief in my ability to overcome any obstacle.

When setbacks came my way, it was crucial to approach them with a positive mindset. Instead of dwelling on the disappointment or frustration, I shifted my focus toward the lessons to be learned from the experience.

CELEBRATING SUCCESS

The road to my success was paved with determination, perseverance, and a willingness to embrace the unknown. It required me to confront my fears and push through the barriers that held me back. No matter how tiny, each step forward was a victory worth acknowledging and cherishing. Celebrating success was not just about the end result; it was about recognizing the effort, growth, and progress I had made. It was about acknowledging the courage it took to step out of my comfort zone and the lessons I learned along the way. It was about appreciating the journey and the person I became because of it.

Celebrating my successes meant infusing myself with renewed motivation and inspiration. I built momentum and confidence, which propelled me forward on my path toward even more remarkable achievements. Acknowledging and appreciating my successes, I cultivated a positive mindset that fueled my continued growth and success. In celebrating success, I not only acknowledged my achievements, but I also honored the journey itself. Recognizing that success was not just a destination but a continuous growth, discovery, and self-improvement process. It was a testament to my resilience, determination, and unwavering belief in myself.

I had an opportunity to celebrate the success of my doctoral journey in May 2023, when I was awarded my degree. I celebrated with family and friends, who were all my support system throughout the process. It is possible to step out of your comfort zone to achieve your greatest goals and walk in God's purpose for your life.

DR. TERESA A. BENNETT

Dr. Teresa A. Bennett is a distinguished educational leader with an illustrious career spanning over three decades. Dr. Teresa is an unwavering authority figure in education, leadership, and dual enrollment. Her journey is a testament to her relentless dedication to shaping education's future and nurturing tomorrow's leaders.

With a career marked by exceptional leadership, Dr. Teresa holds the esteemed position of Educational Consultant at BEC., Dual Enrollment Instructor with Chesterfield County Public Schools, and Adjunct Faculty with Brightpoint Community College. Her role is pivotal in shaping the educational landscape and fostering a nurturing environment for student's growth and development.

Dr. Teresa's academic journey is equally impressive. She holds a bachelor's degree in biology from North Carolina Central University and pursued her master's degree in divinity at Virginia Union University. Her passion for the sciences led her to earn a master's degree in biology from Virginia State University. Dr. Teresa's dedication to educational leadership culminated in a doctorate degree in educational leadership and supervision.

Dr. Teresa is renowned for advocating diversity and inclusion in educational settings. She actively works to create classrooms that embrace diversity, ensuring that all students have an equal opportunity to thrive.

THE COURAGEOUS PATH
OVERCOMING OBSTACLES AND NAVIGATING UNCERTAINTY

SHEYA CHISENGA

L ife as a Christian woman chief executive officer (CEO) is not without its challenges. Along your journey, you will encounter obstacles and face moments of uncertainty. In my chapter, "The Courageous Path: Overcoming Obstacles and Navigating Uncertainty," we will explore the essential tools you need to build resilience, face your fears, learn from failures and setbacks, and develop problem-solving skills. With a courageous spirit, you can navigate through adversity and emerge stronger than ever before.

Building resilience is key to facing the inevitable challenges that come your way. Resilience is the ability to bounce back from setbacks, adapt to change, and maintain a positive outlook amid adversity. As a Christian woman CEO, you can draw strength from your faith and trust in God's plan for your life. Cultivate resilience by nurturing your physical, emotional, and spiritual well-being. Take care of yourself through regular exercise, healthy eating, and self-care practices. Seek support from your faith community, mentors, and loved ones who can offer guidance and encouragement.

Embrace the mindset that setbacks are not permanent, but opportunities for growth and learning. With resilience as your foundation, you can face any obstacle with courage and determination.

In 2021, I felt it was time for my business to evolve and grow, but I needed to figure out how to move forward. I had created sustainable income, but it was not at the level I needed because of the business model and structure I had in place. I began to try different things in the business, creating new programs and various marketing strategies. Still, I kept attracting a specific audience, not at the level of investing at a premium or an elite rate, so my prices stayed low, and I could not grow.

Although I was grateful, I knew God had more for me. I didn't realize that obtaining the next level required another level of commitment in my mindset and my belief in who God had created me to be.

I remember going to an event in Atlanta, Georgia. It was awesome, and I invested at a level that I had never thought I would ever do. It was a high-figure investment, but I trusted God and was all in. Honestly, that was the easy part; the work that came behind that became more intense, but I knew that God was with me. My first thought was, *I'm going to make this money back,* and honestly, I did, But I didn't realize I needed to continue investing at that level. God was calling me, too, and it required a level of faith that had me shaking in my boots. That may sound funny, but I was seriously trembling. Every day, I would cry out to God, and He would give me peace that I was moving in the right direction.

Despite rebranding my business and upgrading my vision and message by the end of 2022, my past and new clients were not as ready to enroll as I had hoped. I kept asking myself what I was doing wrong and sought guidance through prayer and support from my coach. I continued to implement changes and take action toward my goals.

Finally, I launched a new way to serve my clients, and things have begun to turn around. I'm sharing this part of my journey because many of you are already thinking that everything or every idea works, and the truth is they don't, but what they do is they build the leadership skill in you and the faith that you have in God that He is with you. He's making you and who He desires for you to be. So, no, you're not doing anything wrong. God is making you a mighty woman of God and a leader who can support and lead others. It's the journey, not the destination. Our destination continues to evolve because we grow in knowledge and wisdom.

Fear is a natural response when confronted with uncertainty and challenges. However, as a Christian woman CEO, you are called to overcome fear with faith. Trust that God is with you every step of the way and that He has equipped you with the strength to face your fears head-on. Acknowledge your fears, but do not let them dictate your actions. Step out of your comfort zone and embrace new opportunities, even if they seem daunting at first. Surround yourself with a supportive community that uplifts and encourages you in times of fear.

Remember, courage is not the absence of fear, but the willingness to take action despite it. Embrace the courage within you and trust that God's plan is greater than any fear you may encounter.

Failures and setbacks are inevitable in any journey, including your path as a Christian woman CEO. However, it is through these moments of failure that valuable lessons are learned and growth occurs. Embrace failures as stepping stones to success and opportunities for personal and professional development. Reflect on the lessons learned from each setback, and use them as fuel for improvement. Remember, failure does not define you, but how you respond to it does. Lean on your faith to find strength and resilience during these times. Seek support and guidance from mentors and peers who have experienced similar challenges. By learning from your failures and setbacks, you are better equipped to face future obstacles with wisdom and resilience.

Developing problem-solving skills is crucial in navigating the uncertainties that arise in your journey as a Christian woman CEO. Effective problem-solving involves analyzing challenges, identifying possible solutions, and taking decisive action. Approach problems with a growth mindset, viewing them as opportunities for creative thinking and innovation. Seek diverse perspectives, and collaborate with your team to generate innovative solutions. Trust in your ability to find solutions through prayer, discernment, and seeking guidance from God. Remember, problem-solving is not about finding the perfect solution every time, but about taking intentional steps toward progress. Embrace a solution-oriented mindset and trust that with each problem you encounter, you are growing as a leader.

In the face of obstacles and uncertainty, remember that you are not alone on this courageous path. Draw strength from your relationship with God, and trust in His guidance and provision. Seek solace and wisdom through prayer, meditation, and reflection. Allow your faith to be the anchor that keeps you grounded amid the storms of uncertainty.

Surround yourself with a supportive network of fellow Christian businesswomen and mentors who can offer guidance and encouragement during challenging times. Share your experiences and learn from theirs, knowing that their wisdom can help navigate obstacles more effectively. Additionally, consider seeking out professional development opportunities and resources to enhance your problem-solving skills and broaden your perspective.

Ultimately, the courageous path is not about avoiding obstacles or eliminating uncertainty, but about embracing them with faith, resilience, and a problem-solving mindset. Embrace the challenges that come your way, knowing that they are opportunities for growth and transformation. Through resilience, facing fears, learning from failures, and developing problem-solving skills, you can navigate the uncertain terrain of entrepreneurship with grace and strength.

SHEYA CHISENGA

Sheya Chisenga, The Woman Christian CEO, is a speaker, leadership business coach, and sales trainer for women entrepreneurs, coaches, and speakers who are called to make a divine impact with purpose. Sheya is the chief executive officer and founder of It's My Time to Rise Business Institute for Women Leaders and Entrepreneurial Center for Women. With more than fourteen years of entrepreneurship, Sheya has dedicated her life to women CEOs, coaches, and speakers to build a thriving business that changes people's lives and creates financial freedom and a legacy. Sheya's entrepreneurial journey began in 2004 through a direct sales company, which led her to become a certified master life coach in 2009 from Dream Mentors International.

In January 2010, Sheya launched her first coaching practice. In September 2013, she leaped out on faith, officially retiring from Corporate America, and relaunched her full-time coaching business, attracting her ideal clients. They were ready and willing to invest in themselves.

In March 2016, Sheya opened the doors of the Women Entrepreneurial Center for professional businesswomen. The organization has published more than 250 new authors through book anthologies and certified 150 life coaches, helping them launch profitable life coaching businesses.

In 2017, she graduated with her bachelor's degree in Christian studies from Grand Canyon University. She also became an ordained licensed missionary-evangelist through the Church of God in Christ, Inc.

Sheya can teach women how to take their God-given vision and create the life that awaits them by building a purpose-driven coaching company, using their gifts to glorify God, and building multiple six-figure global brands and premium empowerment coaching companies.

Sheya has written five inspiring books. Her most recent is *She Leads, She Profits: Unleashing Bold and Courageous Faith to Become a Full-time CEO*. She has more than twenty-five years of experience conducting workshops, trainings, and speaking. To learn more about Coach Sheya Chisenga, visit www.thewomanchristianceo.com.

BREAKING BARRIERS
A MOTHER-DAUGHTER JOURNEY TO HEALING AND UNDERSTANDING
COURTNEY K. CURTIS

Growing up, my relationship with my mother was challenging. To be honest, we didn't always see eye to eye. The details of my story might not be well known, but sharing it is a path to freedom. Only a few close friends and family truly understood the ups and downs of our connection. From my perspective, my mother often seemed irritable and unkind. While I can't speak to her feelings about me, her actions suggested she viewed me as a spoiled brat. It might be uncomfortable for some to hear this, especially since my mother passed away in 2019. However, I believe in telling my truth to liberate others. Even if it means risking judgment or altering how others perceive me, if my story helps one mother and daughter improve their relationship, it is worth it.

NAVIGATING THE TURBULENCE OF TEENAGE YEARS

Let's rewind to my teenage years—a tumultuous period for my relationship with my mother. In many ways, our struggles were likely similar to other mother-daughter dynamics. With all respect to my mother, I will not write from her view, only mine, but hopefully it can still help both mothers and daughters alike. Let me set the stage for you: As a teenager, I was a pretty good child, made good grades, was in extracurricular activities and even had a job where I saved the money I earned for my gas and school lunch.

I never got in any trouble at school, but home was a bit different. I had a pretty smart mouth when it came to my mother. Her responses often felt frustrated and short, leaving me feeling unheard and unimportant. Although I knew she loved me, the disconnect between feeling loved and wanted created a significant gap in our relationship. I was unable to open up to her due to the fear, judgment, ridicule, and punishment that may come my way.

Reflecting on those times, I wonder about the traumas my mother might have endured. Back then, I couldn't see beyond my own struggles, but now I understand that even the most giving people can face internal challenges.

My mother was a beautiful and sweet person who helped a lot of people in the community. She enjoyed helping those with disabilities and people who had fallen on hard times—whether it be homelessness, mental illness, or abuse. I remember her starting the Abuse Ministry at our church to help those who found themselves in abusive relationships.

I need you to know that even the most giving people can be hurting on the inside and struggling when no one else is around. When that hurt is present, there are only a handful of people—most times those who they live with—who experience the hurt version of them. I wonder if I grew up knowing the hurt version of my mother and not truly getting to see the beautiful side of her that everyone else saw. I inherited my heart for people from her, but I rarely witnessed the side of her that others experienced. Determined to break this cycle of hurt for my children, I've learned that parenting is a mindset not an emotion, one that evolves and brings both challenges and beauty.

THE EVOLVING LANDSCAPE OF PARENTING

Parenting is a state of mind. Parenting can change you from the inside out. It can bring all of the ugly things out of you, and it can bring the most beautiful things out of you too. True to the cliché, parenting does not come with a manual, you just do it! But are you doing it right? Is there a right way? I believe that there is no right way to parent because every child will need something different. The only way you will know if you are doing it right is that your relationship with your child is not altered, mutual respect is preset and the line of communication remains open.

I often think about the result when looking at the goals that I want to reach. As a thoughtful, results oriented, and purposeful parent, every action I do has a purpose and contributes to a positive end goal. So let's talk about a couple of parenting mindsets and the end goal or purpose of each. This is one that you may know or experienced. Let's name it the "Because I Said So" mindset. When thinking about this mindset, I ask myself, what is the purpose or goal of saying, "Because I said so"? Is this contributing to the end goal of creating a better relationship with my child? Or is it creating a bigger wedge between us? Now for your child, this may not be a phrase that bothers them much, but for others, it could very well be. We will talk about how to know this later in the chapter. Now imagine your child asking you "Why do I have to go to Grandma's house today?" Your response in a sharp tone is, "Because I said so!" Now you take a few minutes and figure out at least one related purpose of saying, "Because I said so" to your child.

Okay, so maybe you said, "My child needs to know that I am the one in control" or "They are kids. I don't have to explain myself." Or maybe you said, "I don't have time to explain everything!" Now that you know why you said it, do you feel that it was productive to your overall goals of parenting your child? Was it counterproductive? Do you want to find another way to respond?

I have had to catch myself from saying "Because I said so" quite a few times when my seven-year-old daughter asked me why she had to do something. It is especially hard when your child is not listening and you are frustrated from having to explain yourself...to a *child*. Why should I have to explain myself to a child? Well, there is a certain amount of pride that comes with this saying, and being prideful with your children—really, anyone—is not the best way to handle situations. It will leave your children confused and even more frustrated as to why they can't do what they're asked to do. Children do better with explanations, which will help them make sense of your no and will create an opportunity for you and your child to be in harmony with each other. It is also an opportunity to show them that being open and having a discussion is a valid option in your relationship. Just like you were open and honest with them about your decision, they can be open and honest with you about their feelings and desires.

Imagine a door in their head, and every time you say something counterproductive to your relationship, the door closes. This door closing is a symbol of them closing down their emotions and not being open or communicative with you. But every time you explain something to them, give them a long hug, or tell them you are proud of them, the door swings open. It is still possible for the door to swing open and stay open, but it will take practice from you to keep the door open. Some children may not need explanations or even hugs and affirmations as much, but you will have to observe and know your child to know when certain things are needed.

Being open and transparent with your child most certainly comes with its boundaries. For example, I do not suggest parents overexplain. Provide one explanation to your child and move on. Yes, they still may be upset, but because you have explained your reasoning, they will come around. If they are still questioning why or your explanation doesn't make sense to them, you always have the option of letting them know that they will have to trust you that this is the right decision for them. Let them have their moment, and come back to check on them later, but the last thing you want to do is get frustrated with them. It is also important that parents don't ignore and put off when children are angry or upset. Again, they will need their time and space, but once you feel they will be able to receive it, come back to the situation and talk about it. This creates the open door to talk with your child and let them know you are present for them when they are going through hard times.

At sixteen years and three months old, the minimum age to drive, I received my driver's license. My father gave me a car, and this created the freedom I had wanted for so long. You would have thought that this would create a better relationship with us since most of our issues stemmed from my mother being strict, but unfortunately, the wedge had already been created. I didn't see her as someone I could be open with and tell my problems.

This brings me to another parenting mindset. We will call this one, "We Can't Be Friends" parenting. I feel that this is one that a lot of the black culture can relate to growing up. I believe there is a healthy way to be friends with your child and still have boundaries. I think that a lot of people misconstrue the definition of a friend, so let's define it. A friend is *a person whom one knows and with whom one has a bond of mutual affection.* Do you want to really know your child? Do you want to like your child? Do you want your child to feel a genuine warmth and kindness from you? If yes, then surprise! You want to be friends with your child. I know, this is opposite from what you grew up learning. Same.

It is easy to see why someone would not want to be "friends" with their child. Again, that term *friend* gets misconstrued very quickly, and people think that a friend is just someone who you go out, have fun with on the weekends, and tell your deepest desires to. I can see why parents would have this particular mindset. There are parents who say that their children are their friends but have no boundaries in the relationship, which leads to unhealthy and misbehaved children. Growing up, I was familiar with a mother and daughter who were extremely close. The child was never reprimanded, often made her own decisions on important life choices without the mother even caring to know the decision, and smoked with her parent. This type of relationship between parent and child can create children who are defiant, have no respect for adults or authority, and make horrible life decisions. Boundaries are important.

 Is it possible to be a friend to your child and have set boundaries?

Absolutely! First, just like any friendship, parents have to learn their children. There is a right way to discipline your child. There is a right way to speak to your child. There is a right way to show love to your child, but these are all things you have to learn. You learn this by observing your children as they grow. Learn their personality, what they like and dislike, as well as understanding how they treat others, and learning their love language. Once you know these things, implement them into your relationship. Just like any other relationship/friendship, there will be valleys. In the valleys, communicate. If it is hard to communicate, find a family therapist that can help with communication, but *always* attempt to keep your line of communication open. Think of that door swinging open.

Once you implement the right discipline, the right tone and words, and the correct love language for your child, the next step is to...*have fun.* Show your child that you can laugh, joke, and have fun around them. What is a friendship without laughter? Go on special one-on-one dates. Make your dates consistent. Being a friend to your child is possible with boundaries. It is important to write down your boundaries and keep them.

What are boundaries as a parent? It will vary from parent to parent. Here are some of mine: I don't share any problems between my husband and me with my children. My belief is that children's view of their parents should not be skewed in a negative way because of the relationship that their parents may have with each other. I don't allow attitudes between my children. They have no choice but to get along. My husband and I teach them that one day we will be gone, and they will have to lean on each other. We allow them their moments, but they have to come back and apologize or talk about their issues with their siblings. Simple boundaries include decent bedtimes, chores around the home, and teaching my kids to give space to others when it is needed.

PARENTING THROUGH MENTAL HEALTH

Parenting especially comes with its woes when you have a child who is experiencing mental health issues. I was never diagnosed with depression, but I definitely had my moments of depression and suicidal thoughts as a teenager. There are so many discussions around mental health now, but when I was a teenager, it was the opposite. Going to a therapist in the nineties was for teenagers who were experiencing extreme behaviors, not for a teenager who had occasional hard times.

I remember a time where my mother and I were in another heated argument. I pulled a knife from the kitchen and demanded she move out of my way. I ran out of the house and had a friend come pick me up. I ended up staying at a family member's home for the night because I knew my family would be worried if I just disappeared. My relationship with my mother had gotten to a terrible point, and at that time, there were no outlets for me. There was no one to talk to, and I felt a great deal of blame, resentment, embarrassment, and fear. Some of the closest people to me didn't even know what was going on in my head. It was something I just had to get over and live through. My only saving grace was God and my relationship with Him.

Do you know what is going through your child's mind? Does your child have an outlet or someone to talk to?

Our company, Family Services, Inc., serves children and adolescents who go through traumatic pasts and, as a result, have extreme and challenging behaviors. We provide resources for the children and families and an outlet for the children. Most of the times, the children just need to know that someone cares and will listen to them. We connect them to an outpatient therapist, psychiatrist, and case manager, if needed, and sit with them two to three times a week to go over ways to handle difficult situations better. These services are a true gem to the relationship between parents and children, but at times, there are changes that the parents need to make as well. This is where our parent coaching has come in to provide tips and advice on parenting their children and connecting them to resources such as an outpatient therapist.

As a company, we believe that is important that parents find, understand, and heal from their trauma so that they can parent healthily.

EXCUSES AS A PARENT

Do we have excuses as parents? Of course we do. We are human first, but in order to help our children, we have to heal. Sometimes we have to sit in our emotions, let the healing come, and use our emotions as a ladder to our resilience in parenting. Certainly our goal should be to not have any excuses, but you cannot do this without first learning and practicing.

I had three kids calling me at one time—my seven-, four-, and three-year-old. I had one on my leg asking for a snack, the other needing homework help, and the other wanting me to watch her flip. Everything in me wanted to yell and tell them all to be quiet and sit down. Instead I sat in my emotion. Oftentimes we will want to feed and satisfy our emotions by screaming, stomping, and having a reaction. Have you ever just sat in your emotion until it went away—I mean, did absolutely nothing? It's a hard thing to do, but I think of it as leveling up in a game. You can't level up until you pass the current level. In this case, the levels are your emotions. Once you are able to sit in your emotion and feel better without a reaction, then you level up. The next time, it won't be so bad. Your patience will become more and more resilient. That's why the Lord says be quick to listen and slow to speak and slow to become angry. Learn to sit in your emotion. Don't say anything, just feel it.

I will often talk to myself as I sit through it—*Courtney, you can do this.* I play out the scenario of me yelling at my children and the guilt that will come from it. I breathe. I start to distract myself with doing something else. Once my emotion is mostly faded, I congratulate myself. If it is an issue I need to come back to, I come back at a time that is right, when my child will receive it and I can talk calmly and with wisdom.

After graduating from college, I came home, and my mom and my relationship had gotten better but not at all the mother/daughter relationship I desired. It was really hard for me to talk to my mother, let alone have a relationship with her. I always felt like the door was never open for me to talk to her. It was a weird feeling of fear, judgment, dislike, and being really uncomfortable. I moved out and bought a home shortly after moving in with my mother. I felt that it was best for our relationship.

Life went really fast, and before I knew it, I was married with a child, my stepdad had passed away, and we were moving back into my mother's house to be with her after his passing. Having moved back in the home with my mother was a true blessing from God, and let me tell you why: During this time, it was the closest I had ever been to my mother. We had our valleys, but the mixture of losing my stepfather and having a new baby in the house brought us times where we could break down the barriers that had been built up between us.

In November 2018, my mom and I had a huge disagreement about our family dog whom had moved in with us to my mother's home. My mother was pretty much fed up that the dog kept scratching up her floor. From that disagreement, I was fed up. I felt that she constantly complained about the house and how we didn't treat it as if it was ours. I decided to write a letter to her about everything that I had felt from childhood on up. It was quite lengthy, but I needed to tell her. She read my letter, and we were able to talk about it—finally. This was a conversation we had needed for years. It was a release for both of us, and I was so excited to see a giant wall come down in our relationship.

Sadly, in January 2019, my mother passed. I believe that God knew it would be hard for me to move forward after her passing if I had not had the chance to have this conversation with her. It still makes me sad that we were so close to having the mother/daughter relationship that I desired. I knew 2019 would be different for us—movie dates, talking over dinner about marriage and life and whether she felt she would date again. Well that year did not turn out to be how I wanted it, and God had to really bring me through it.

This may sound weird, but I feel my mother with me more now than I ever have. When she passed, I kept her business and legacy alive, and every time I walk through the doors of Family Services Inc., I feel her presence. She is with me.

My belief is that with every generation should come growth. I am actively engaged in the process of acknowledging and understanding my own trauma and seeking ways to create a different experience for my children. Although I am still in the learning phase and occasionally make mistakes, I use those moments as valuable lessons to improve. I refuse to let guilt overwhelm me because I recognize my imperfections. My commitment is to consistently strive for the well-being of my children.

I want you to take this away: Your child needs you present and involved. Whether you use the tips I have provided you or research your own, I guarantee you that your child will benefit from having an open line of communication with you, and it may even save their life.

When it comes to creating an open line of communication with your child, there are *no* excuses. So, what will you do to be a better parent and have your child be comfortable communicating with you?

COURTNEY CURTIS

Courtney Curtis, a prominent figure in Petersburg, Virginia, is the dynamic force behind Family Services Inc., a thriving mental health agency, and an accomplished local realtor. Hailing from Chesterfield County, Virginia, Courtney's journey reflects a remarkable trajectory marked by profound achievements and a commitment to community well-being.

A graduate of Matoaca High School in 2007, Courtney pursued her higher education at Marymount University, earning a bachelor of science in business administration in 2011. Her early venture into real estate investment emerged during her post-college years, recognizing the numerous advantages it presented. At the age of twenty-three, she acquired her first home, subsequently transforming it into a successful rental property, unveiling her innate expertise for real estate endeavors.

The allure of the real estate industry intensified, leading Courtney to pivot her career, initially embracing part-time real estate endeavors in 2015. Her passion and dedication lead her transition to a full-time realtor in 2017, garnering acclaim and numerous awards for exceptional service and remarkable accomplishments in real estate. Courtney and her husband, Kennard, also showcased their skills by renovating and reselling multiple properties, further solidifying their expertise in the field.

In a significant turn of events in 2019, Courtney inherited Family Services Inc., a mental health agency, from her late mother, Bernetta Quinn. Motivated by their passion for helping youth, Courtney and Kennard redefined the agency's course. They expanded its services to encompass a wide range tailored to adolescents, young adults, and families, including offerings like intensive in home, therapeutic day treatment, therapeutic mentoring, parent coaching, and parent group services.

Courtney's vision for Family Services Inc. is ambitious, aiming to introduce more mental health services to benefit the community, along with establishing a dedicated community center in Petersburg. A devoted mother to three beautiful children and a loving dog, Courtney finds solace in family, work, nature walks, and exploring new destinations. Her guiding scripture, 2 Corinthians 12:9, underlies her resilience and unwavering determination in navigating both personal and professional spheres.

Courtney Curtis's unwavering dedication to behavioral health, real estate, and community development stands as a testament to her versatile expertise and her commitment to making a meaningful impact in the lives of those she serves.

THE BATTLE OVER ONE'S MIND

THE MENTAL HEALTH STRUGGLE

TIA M. JONES

In the African-American community, there has long been a stigma surrounding mental health, and this stigma persists in society at large. The lack of awareness is a significant barrier, as many individuals with mental illness may not even be aware of their condition. This lack of self-awareness is compounded by the absence of support from family members or loved ones, creating a challenging environment for those grappling with mental health issues.

Fear and distrust further contribute to the reluctance to confide in others about mental health struggles. Additionally, financial concerns can act as a hindrance to seeking professional help. The prevailing stigma and discrimination toward people with mental illness make it difficult to have open and transparent conversations about mental well-being. Consequently, individuals often downplay their struggles or face derogatory labels such as "crazy" or "retarded."

Studies indicate that women are more likely to suffer from mental illness, yet men are less inclined to seek treatment. Early intervention is crucial, as untreated signs and symptoms of mental illness can worsen over time. However, addressing mental illnesses is complex, as it involves more than taking a pill; it requires a nuanced and multifaceted approach.

Half of mental illnesses manifest by the age of fourteen, often presenting as behavioral problems. Stress, when not managed effectively, can escalate into emotional outbursts, creating a barrier to understanding the underlying issues individuals face. Unfortunately, the Black community often faces challenges in accessing mental health treatment due to concerns about judgment and potential mistreatment.

The harmful effects of social media, exposure to racism, mental health stigma, and cumulative trauma contribute to the alarming suicide rates in the African-American community. Suicide is the second leading cause of death for Black youths aged ten to nineteen and young adults aged twenty to twenty-six.

Personal experiences underscore the urgency of addressing mental health issues within the community. At the onset of 2022, as the new year unfolded and life progressed, the day following my son's twenty-third birthday marked a heartbreaking moment. I received one of the most devastating phone calls of my life. Amid the background echoes of his mother's anguished cries, a close friend delivered the heart-wrenching news to me: The young man whom I had cherished since his childhood, growing up alongside my own kids and affectionately calling me Auntie, was no more. He had taken his own life just after joining my son and their friends the night before to celebrate my son's birthday. The surreal nature of this reality was beyond anything I could have fathomed in a thousand years.

This tragedy happened around the same time of actress Regina King's son and Miss USA 2019 Cheslie Kryst, highlighting the pressing need for open dialogue and support systems. It is essential to shift the narrative around mental health, recognizing that mental illnesses are not just "craziness" but legitimate health concerns. Even with the experience I have as a mental health provider, this event was something I never imagined to happen to someone I loved so dearly.

Research indicates that Blacks are twenty percent more likely to experience serious mental health problems. These problems encompass various disorders, including major depressive disorder, generalized anxiety disorder, bipolar disorder, and trauma and stress-related disorders. Childhood traumas often carry over into adulthood, impacting mental health and triggering various disorders.

The reluctance to address mental health concerns until a crisis occurs is a prevalent issue. Childhood traumas, if left unaddressed, can lead to negative coping mechanisms, and in extreme cases, a mental health crisis. In these situations, individuals may require external assistance to access the help they need.

Psychiatric emergencies, including suicidal thoughts, violence, agitation, substance abuse delirium, severe depression, and psychosis with suicidal or homicidal tendencies, underscore the urgency of addressing mental health issues proactively. Encouraging open conversations, eliminating stigma, and reframing mental health discussions are crucial steps in preventing tragic outcomes and ensuring individuals receive the support they need.

As someone with more than twenty years of experience in mental health, the importance of raising awareness and providing support for mental health in the African-American community cannot be overstated. By promoting understanding, empathy, and accessible mental health resources, we can work toward a future where mental well-being is prioritized and stigma is eradicated.

The intricate web of challenges surrounding mental health in the African-American community requires a comprehensive and nuanced approach. Beyond the statistics and broad strokes, delving into the specific factors exacerbating mental health disparities is essential to crafting effective solutions.

One critical factor is the historical context that has shaped attitudes toward mental health within the African-American community. The enduring legacy of systemic racism, discrimination, and inequality has contributed to a culture where mental health concerns are often stigmatized or dismissed. The intergenerational trauma stemming from experiences like slavery, segregation, and systemic oppression has created a complex backdrop for mental health conversations.

In addition to historical factors, socioeconomic disparities play a significant role. Access to mental health resources is often limited in marginalized communities, compounding the challenges individuals face. The financial burden associated with seeking professional help, coupled with a shortage of mental health providers in many communities, creates substantial barriers to care.

Education also emerges as a crucial aspect. There is a need for widespread awareness campaigns that debunk myths surrounding mental health and dismantle the pervasive stigma. Culturally competent education that recognizes the unique experiences of African Americans is vital to fostering understanding and encouraging early intervention.

Moreover, gender norms and expectations within the community can influence how mental health is perceived and addressed. Traditional notions of masculinity may discourage men from expressing vulnerability or seeking help, perpetuating a cycle of untreated mental health issues. Addressing these gender dynamics is essential for creating an environment where everyone feels empowered to prioritize their mental well-being.

The impact of external factors, such as exposure to violence and racism, cannot be understated. These stressors contribute significantly to the high prevalence of mental health challenges in the African-American community. Recognizing and addressing the intersectionality of these factors is key to providing holistic support.

Building a robust mental health infrastructure tailored to the needs of the African-American community is imperative. This involves not only increasing the availability of affordable mental health services but also training professionals who understand the cultural nuances and historical context that shape individuals' experiences.

Furthermore, community-based initiatives can play a pivotal role in normalizing mental health conversations. Establishing safe spaces where individuals can share their experiences without fear of judgment is crucial. Encouraging community leaders, influencers, and educators to openly discuss their own mental health journeys can break down barriers and inspire others to seek help.

In the quest for systemic change, collaboration between mental health professionals, community leaders, and policymakers is essential. Advocacy for policies that address socioeconomic disparities, increase funding for mental health services, and promote mental health education can contribute to creating a more supportive environment.

Ultimately, the journey toward improved mental health in the African-American community requires a multifaceted and collaborative effort. By addressing the unique challenges rooted in history, culture, and socioeconomics, we can pave the way for a future where mental health is prioritized, stigma is eradicated, and everyone has equal access to the support they need.

Exploring the complex landscape of mental health within the African-American community demands a deeper understanding of the multifaceted challenges and potential solutions. Beyond the systemic issues, there are nuanced cultural dynamics and community-specific stressors that shape the mental health narrative.

Historically, the African-American community has developed resilient coping mechanisms in the face of adversity. However, these coping mechanisms often involve suppressing emotions or enduring suffering silently, contributing to the stigma surrounding mental health. Breaking through this cultural norm requires a delicate balance of acknowledging the strength ingrained in the community while fostering a culture that encourages open dialogue about mental well-being.

Moreover, religious and spiritual beliefs play a significant role in the lives of many within the African-American community. While faith can be a source of strength, it may also contribute to the stigma around seeking professional mental health support. Integrating mental health discussions within the framework of spirituality and emphasizing that seeking help aligns with personal and spiritual growth is crucial.

Socioeconomic disparities intersect with cultural factors, creating a unique set of challenges. Economic instability, limited access to quality education, and systemic barriers to employment opportunities can lead to chronic stressors that exacerbate mental health issues. Addressing mental health within the African-American community necessitates a holistic approach that includes economic empowerment, education reform, and social justice initiatives.

The role of family and community support cannot be overstated. In many instances, family units serve as the primary source of emotional sustenance. However, familial dynamics can also perpetuate silence and inhibit open discussions about mental health. Encouraging families to become allies in the mental health journey involves dismantling generational patterns and fostering environments where vulnerability is met with understanding and support.

Creating culturally competent mental health services is a pivotal step in breaking down the barriers to care. Training mental health professionals to understand the cultural nuances, historical context, and unique experiences of the African-American community is essential. This includes recognizing the impact of racial trauma and providing trauma-informed care that acknowledges the systemic injustices individuals may have faced.

Community-driven initiatives that emphasize peer support, mentorship programs, and grassroots advocacy can be transformative. Establishing safe spaces within communities where individuals can share their stories, exchange coping strategies, and find solidarity is crucial. Community leaders, influencers, and educators can play a pivotal role in normalizing conversations around mental health by sharing their own journeys and emphasizing that seeking help is a courageous act.

In the broader societal context, dispelling harmful stereotypes and challenging discriminatory practices is imperative. Media representation that accurately portrays the diversity of experiences within the African-American community can contribute to reshaping public perceptions of mental health. Additionally, policy advocacy that addresses the root causes of systemic inequalities, including equitable access to healthcare and socioeconomic opportunities, is fundamental.

Ultimately, fostering mental health resilience within the African-American community requires a collaborative and intersectional approach. By recognizing and addressing cultural nuances, historical legacies, and systemic injustices, we can work toward a future where mental health is prioritized, stigma is dismantled, and all individuals have the support they need to thrive.

The issue of mental health in the Black community is deeply complex and fraught with challenges. Historically, societal stigmas have been attached to mental illness, creating barriers to both awareness and support. This lack of understanding often means that those suffering may not even recognize their own struggles, compounded by fears of judgment or distrust in confiding in others. Financial constraints can further limit access to necessary care.

In this context, the experiences of trauma and its long-term effects are particularly heart-wrenching. Consider a young girl losing her mother early, subjected to incest, and left without any psychological support or justice. This trauma, unaddressed, can ripple through generations, as evidenced by the recurring patterns of abuse within families. These narratives are not isolated; they are part of a broader tapestry of mental health issues that are too often neglected.

Post-traumatic stress disorder (PTSD) stemming from various forms of trauma, including sexual abuse, violence, and emotional mistreatment, is a significant concern. It persists over time, severely impairing daily functioning. Treatment options include individual and group therapy and, when necessary, medication for associated conditions like insomnia, anxiety, depression, and substance abuse, which often arises as a maladaptive coping mechanism in response to unaddressed mental health issues, leading to a cycle of neglect and deterioration in social, professional, and educational contexts.

In the Black community, there is a pressing need for a paradigm shift in how mental health is approached and understood. Despite the prevalence of mental disorders, cultural narratives often dismiss these serious concerns as mere eccentricities or weaknesses. This misunderstanding can prevent individuals from seeking help and receiving the support they need.

The impact of social media, exposure to racism, and ongoing trauma play significant roles in mental health and have been linked to increased rates of suicide, particularly among Black youths. Warning signs, such as substance abuse, a lack of purpose, withdrawal from society, uncontrolled anger, and risk-taking behaviors, are critical indicators of a deeper crisis.

From my two decades of experience in mental health, I've witnessed firsthand the breadth of these issues. It's clear that more awareness and support are needed to treat mental health with the same urgency as physical health. The alarming rates of suicide, particularly among young Black males, LGBTQ+ youths, and those with a family history of mental disorders, underscore the urgency of this issue.

The relationship between mental health and suicide is complex and often rooted in a combination of difficult life events and mental disorders. Individuals may experience overwhelming despair, severe anxiety, and psychosis, leading them to consider suicide as an escape from pain.

To address this crisis, it is vital to provide comprehensive psychiatric care, including emergency interventions like emergency custody orders (ECO) and temporary detention orders (TDO). Treatment should encompass a variety of modalities, supervised and evaluated by medical professionals to cater to the specific needs and severity of each case.

As a community, we must advocate for those suffering from mental health issues, encouraging them to seek help and supporting them through their journey. It's crucial to reframe the conversation around mental health, recognizing warning signs, and intervening before it's too late. This shift in perspective and action can make a profound difference in addressing mental health challenges in the Black community.

After seeing the intricacies and challenges in the care and treatment of individuals with mental health issues, it becomes evident that this matter demands attention not just at the local level but also nationally. One of the significant obstacles to receiving adequate care is insurance limitations. Often, individuals are not fully stabilized but are discharged due to insurance constraints, leaving them to fend for themselves prematurely. This situation is far from ideal, as it can lead to repeated cycles of crisis and intervention without long-term resolution.

For those experiencing severe mental health crises, being taken under a TDO to a mental hospital for evaluation and treatment is sometimes the only option. With the rising rates of suicide and increasing mental health–related incidents, immediate and effective intervention becomes crucial. In healthcare settings like doctors' offices or emergency rooms, when someone expresses thoughts of depression, self-harm, or harming others, healthcare professionals are legally required to initiate an ECO for emergency commitment. However, this process can be challenging, as many individuals struggling with addiction or mental health issues may be in denial about their condition or hesitant to seek help.

This is where the role of family members and close acquaintances becomes vital. They can encourage their loved ones to seek help, but it's essential to approach these situations sensitively to avoid creating communication barriers. Trust is a significant factor in these scenarios, and many people with mental health issues may have difficulty trusting others, including healthcare professionals.

Therefore, we need to foster an environment where seeking help for mental health issues is normalized and encouraged. It is crucial to be the voice for those suffering and advocating for their needs. We must believe individuals who express their struggles and take their words seriously. Reframing the conversation around mental health in our communities is essential, moving away from stigma and toward understanding and support.

Ignoring the signs and red flags of mental health issues can no longer be an option. It's not always a comfortable topic, but avoiding it only exacerbates the problem. Addressing mental health stigma head-on and ensuring that individuals get the help they need is a matter of urgency.

As we look at this approach, it is not just about treating illnesses; it's about saving lives and improving the quality of life for countless individuals and their families.

In conclusion, a collective effort is required to change the narrative around mental health. This includes educating communities, improving access to care, advocating for better policies and insurance coverages, and creating a supportive and understanding environment. By doing so, we can make significant strides in addressing mental health issues effectively and compassionately.

TIA M. JONES

Tia M. Jones, a dedicated mother of two sons, Jahquan and Deonte Harris, has profoundly impacted mental health throughout her career. Her journey began at Central State Hospital Forensic Unit immediately after high school, and since then, she has tirelessly devoted herself to helping individuals with various disabilities, children, and adults with autism. Her educational pursuits at Brightpoint Community College in Human Services have enriched her expertise.

As an expert mental health specialist, Tia's unwavering commitment to mental health care shines brightly. Tia's extensive knowledge and steadfast dedication establish her as an esteemed authority in this pivotal field. Beyond her contributions to mental health, Tia demonstrates leadership and excellence in the healthcare sector. Her active engagement in mandatory training underscores her unwavering commitment to professional excellence.

Tia's leadership prowess is further evident as a former customer service representative. Her interactions with individuals seeking information about their accounts are marked by an unwavering dedication to delivering top-notch customer satisfaction. Her adherence to company rules and regulations underscores her reputation as an exemplary professional in the corporate realm.

Tia Harris is an authority in the mental health domain and an esteemed leader across various spheres, including healthcare, corporate leadership, and empowerment. Her journey is characterized by empowerment, unwavering dedication, and an unbeatable commitment to enriching the lives of others. Tia's influence transcends diverse fields, highlighting her exceptional leadership and expertise.

INTERLOCKING ESSENCE

THE PUZZLE PIECES OF A TRANSFORMATIVE JOURNEY

DR. VALARIE W. HARRIS

PROPEL INTO THE NEXT

Stepping beyond your comfort zone is a profound journey, and my own experiences have been a testament to the transformative power of embracing discomfort. My story is not just a narrative but a reflection of the principles I advocate for in personal and professional development.

I stopped allowing bad experiences, circumstances, obstacles, and people to dictate my future. I vividly recall a moment in my life and career where I felt the need for growth and expansion. It was a pivotal point that demanded a departure from the familiar and a leap into the unknown. With a contagious drive and a commitment to my own mantra that I have greatness inside of me that the world needs, I embarked on a journey that would redefine my professional and personal path.

One of the concrete, achievable steps I took was to immerse myself in new opportunities and challenges. Instead of shying away from unfamiliar territories, I actively sought them out. This action-oriented approach allowed me to confront fears, uncertainties, and doubts head-on. During this journey, I found solace in thought-provoking questions that invited introspection. Questions such as, "What is holding me back?" and "How can I leverage my potential for greater impact?" became guiding lights, thrusting me forward on my path of growth.

PIVOTAL MOMENTS IN LIFE

As a young girl, the dream of visiting Africa was a constant whisper in the corridors of my imagination. Little did I know that it would take sixty-four years for this cherished dream to unfold into a tangible reality. Stepping beyond the boundaries of my comfort zone marked a pivotal moment in my life as I embarked on a transformative journey with Uniquely Chosen Ministries to engage in missions in Ghana, West Africa. Despite holding a passport adorned with stamps from various destinations, the prospect of realizing a childhood dream added a layer of excitement to the travel preparations.

The anticipation reached its zenith as I secured the necessary shots, completed the requisite applications, and obtained my visa, signaling that the momentous journey was imminent. The realization that I was on the cusp of visiting a land where my roots extend, where my people continue to thrive, was a surreal and exhilarating experience.

Upon landing in Ghana, the stark contrasts in culture, culinary delights, and social customs were immediately apparent. Yet, amid these differences, the warmth and love exuded by the people enveloped us from the outset. The gracious reception we received at the airport, the dedicated individuals who accompanied and assisted us throughout our stay, exemplified the hospitality that became synonymous with our Ghanaian experience.

Under the adept leadership of our guide, the meticulously planned trip allowed us to distribute essential supplies to various schools. Witnessing the joy and gratitude of children who eagerly accepted our gifts left an indelible mark on my heart. Their radiant smiles and expressions of thanks linger in my memory, a testament to the impact even small gestures can have on young lives.

As a worshiper, my encounter with the vibrant and unscripted worship in Africa was a revelation. The singing and dancing were not merely expressions of faith; they were profound manifestations of genuine, unfiltered worship. Despite the challenging conditions— walking for miles to reach the house of the Lord, standing on dirt floors with no windows—the hunger for God's presence was palpable. The worship experience transcended circumstances, reminding me of the universal connection we share through faith.

During this extraordinary journey, I had the privilege of not only attending worship services but also preaching and conducting a leadership workshop for women. Stepping out of my comfort zone required adapting to the use of an interpreter, slowing down my pace during ministry, and navigating unfamiliar dynamics. Yet, in these challenges, I found God's faithfulness guiding me through an extraordinary encounter.

This experience underscored the understanding that stepping beyond one's comfort zone is not a one-time event but a lifelong journey, presenting itself in different phases of life. There is no predetermined rhythm or rhyme to this process; it demands a willingness to step out in faith. I stand here today to encourage you to venture into the unknown, to pursue dreams within arm's reach. You possess the innate ability to initiate the process—just take that first step, for you have the strength to embark on a new adventure in your life.

THE WRITING NARRATIVE

Embarking on my third journey to Africa marked another significant step beyond my comfort zone, one that delved into the realm of my newfound love for writing. From my early days as a child, I found solace and joy in putting pen to paper, crafting stories in my diary during moments of solitude. Despite being labeled as not a good writer by those around me, I continued this practice, unknowingly nurturing a passion that would later transform my life.

God's divine guidance became unmistakably clear to me during my devotions, leading me to write a forty-day journal titled *Talk Time with God*. This endeavor marked the inception of my writing journey, a journey that has since blossomed into eight books, written or contributed to, since the transformative year of 2019. As I reflect on this, I marvel at the realization that, at the age of seventy, I am still fearlessly stepping beyond my comfort zone to pursue dreams that aim to inspire and uplift others in their own life journeys.

Writing has become a potent tool through which I illustrate the concepts that have shaped my life. Drawing from personal experiences and weaving them into relatable narratives, I endeavor to connect with others on a deeply personal level. My stories serve as a testament to the belief that the path to greatness often requires confronting challenges and breaking free from the familiar confines of comfort.

Throughout this transformative process, I have seamlessly integrated scriptures and quotes from inspirational figures. These elements not only add depth and wisdom to my insights, but also serve as powerful motivators during moments of uncertainty. The infusion of these timeless words of wisdom reinforce my conviction that the pursuit of personal empowerment is a journey worth undertaking.

The decision to embrace discomfort, acknowledge the greatness within, and take bold steps beyond my comfort zone has proven to be profoundly rewarding. My journey stands as a living testament to the incredible rewards awaiting those who dare to push their boundaries and embark on the transformative path of personal growth and change. As I continue to navigate this journey, I am fueled by the belief that everyone has the capacity to unleash their greatness and embrace a life of purpose, transcending the limitations of comfort for the boundless possibilities that lie beyond.

LET'S BE FOR REAL

Think about this for a moment: Have you ever realized that your comfort zone could significantly hinder your future success and destiny? It's true. I can attest to staying within the confines of my comfort zone, and it hindered my growth and kept me from surpassing my current reality. We all feel secure within this zone, where routine and familiarity reign. When we become accustomed to doing things a certain way, we often resist making changes, finding ourselves stuck in a self-imposed comfort prison. Despite potential personal and spiritual growth, we can fear what might happen if we step beyond that place of complacency.

Often, even when it's clear that change is part of God's plan for our lives, we choose the safe option, opting for familiarity over the unknown. It's an everyday struggle to settle for what's easy and routine rather than striving for the best God has in store for us. Just like the story of the spy faced with the choice of a firing squad or a big black door, we often choose the known over the unknown. Yet, behind that big black door is freedom, a passage leading outside. Few are brave enough to see what lies beyond.

What is your "big black door"? Has the fear of the unknown trapped you in your comfort zone? To be free from the prison we've created, all we need to do is open the door. Stepping beyond our comfort zone allows us to embrace the destiny God has planned for us, becoming part of the great adventure He has in store. However, it's essential to identify the walls and barriers we've erected around our comfort zones. Have you put up fences preventing you from escaping? What additional barriers are holding you back from the direction God is calling you to take?

This is real talk right here. Sometimes sins from our past can keep us stuck in our comfort zones. However, Isaiah 43:25 reminds us that God blots out our transgressions and doesn't keep a list of our sins. We're encouraged to forget the past and press forward toward the goals God has set for us. So, where is your comfort zone, and where are you in your spiritual walk with God? Take a moment to reflect on whether you're stuck in your comfort zone or stepping out in faith. Are you missing out on the blessings and abundant life Jesus promised because you refuse to leave your comfort zone?

Throughout history, God has taken people from beyond their comfort zones, leading to changed lives, blessings, and accomplishing the impossible. All it takes is a step of faith, leaving the comfort zone behind. Let's not take for granted the beautiful things God is doing in our lives, families, churches, and communities. It's time to leave our comfort zones and step into the life God has called us to live. Are you ready to answer God's call to step beyond your comfort zone and do more incredible things for Him? This is just a reminder from Psalm 37:23, "The Lord directs a person's steps, and the Lord delights in his way."

SEVEN BENEFITS TO STEPPING BEYOND YOUR COMFORT ZONE

1. **Personal Growth:** Stepping beyond your comfort zone is an incentive for personal growth. It challenged me to acquire new skills, gain fresh perspectives, and discover hidden

strengths, fostering a continuous journey of self-improvement.

2. **Increased Resilience:** It helped me to face unfamiliar situations to build resilience. Embracing challenges and overcoming obstacles outside your comfort zone equips you with the mental and emotional strength to handle adversity, both in your personal and professional life.

3. **Expanded Creativity:** Stepping into the unknown helped me to stimulate hidden creativity. Unique experiences force your brain to make new connections and think in different ways, enhancing your ability to generate innovative ideas and solutions.

4. **Enhanced Confidence:** Successfully navigating unfamiliar territory helped me to boost my confidence. Each step outside your comfort zone reinforces the belief that you can overcome challenges, empowering you to tackle more significant opportunities with assurance.

5. **Improved Decision-Making:** Confronting uncertainties sharpens your decision-making skills. Beyond your comfort zone, you learn to analyze situations, weigh risks, and make informed choices, honing your ability to navigate complex scenarios.

6. **Broadened Perspectives:** Exposure to diverse experiences broadens your perspective. Stepping outside your comfort zone allows you to interact with different people, cultures, and ideas, fostering a more inclusive and open-minded worldview.

7. **Achievement of Goals:** Stepping beyond your comfort zone often involves setting and achieving challenging goals. As you successfully accomplish these milestones, you develop a sense of accomplishment and fulfillment, motivating you to pursue even loftier aspirations.

As the narrative unfolds about the transformative benefits of stepping beyond the comfort zone, it becomes apparent that the essence of our lives is intricately woven with a myriad of puzzle pieces. Just as each step outside the comfort zone contributes to personal growth, resilience, creativity, confidence, improved decision-making, broadened perspectives, and the achievement of goals, these life puzzle pieces work in harmony to craft a narrative of holistic fulfillment and purpose. Let's examine how these interconnected aspects, like a carefully assembled puzzle, create a tapestry that transcends the boundaries of the familiar, beckoning us toward a life of depth, meaning, and continual exploration.

PUZZLE PIECES THAT MAKE UP THE ESSENCE OF OUR LIFE

What I have discovered is that life is an intricate pattern of diverse puzzle pieces that collectively shape our existence. Among these pieces are the profound elements of spirituality, family bonds, career aspirations, financial stability, physical and mental well-being, personal and professional development, community engagement, and an enduring commitment to lifelong learning. Much like a puzzle, these components interlock, forming a resilient foundation upon which our lives unfold. Our connection with God provides guidance and purpose, family offers unwavering support, and a flourishing career intertwines with financial stability—health and wellness act as cornerstones, fostering the energy needed to pursue personal and professional growth. Engaging with communities and embracing continual learning contributes to the dynamic nature of this puzzle, propelling us to explore beyond the familiar contours of our comfort zone. Together, these pieces craft a vivid picture, illustrating the intricate beauty of a life woven with intention, connection, and perpetual evolution.

Now imagine your life as a dynamic puzzle, with each piece representing a fundamental aspect: When I look back over my life, I begin to understand how these interconnected pieces serve as catalysts that propelled me beyond my comfort zone.

GOD

Spiritual Courage: Our faith provides strength and courage, encouraging us to trust that we are destined to take bold steps beyond our comfort zone.

FAMILY

Unconditional Support: Having a supportive family becomes our safety net, offering encouragement and reassurance as we move into unfamiliar territory, fostering the confidence to explore new opportunities.

CAREER

Professional Growth: My various vocations became a platform for continual growth. By embracing challenges and seeking new opportunities, it gives us the opportunity to expand our skillset and professional capabilities.

FINANCES

Risk-Taking Capacity: When we have sound financial management, it provides a solid foundation, allowing us the freedom to take calculated risks and explore ventures that may have otherwise seemed daunting.

HEALTH AND WELLNESS

Physical Resilience: The power to have good health enhances our physical and mental resilience, empowering us to handle the stress and uncertainties associated with stepping beyond our comfort zone.

PERSONAL AND PROFESSIONAL DEVELOPMENT

Skill Empowerment: Continuous learning equips us with the skills needed to tackle new challenges, fostering a mindset of adaptability and innovation.

COMMUNITY

Social Support: Engaging with our community creates a network of like-minded individuals who can provide encouragement, advice, and shared experiences, making the journey outside our comfort zone less solitary.

LIFELONG LEARNING

Adaptability: Lifelong learning is the engine of adaptability. It allows us to stay relevant, open to change, and ready to embrace new perspectives and opportunities.

As we assemble these puzzle pieces in harmony, they become a powerful force propelling us beyond our comfort zone. The synergy of these aspects reinforces each other, providing a holistic sense of empowerment that transcends individual boundaries. With a solid foundation in faith, family, and community, we develop the courage to make decisions that lead to growth, both personally and professionally.

The interconnected puzzle pieces encourage purposeful exploration, enabling us to step into unknown territories with a sense of purpose and direction. The journey beyond our comfort zone becomes not just a challenge but a fulfilling transformation where we discover new facets of ourselves, achieve goals, and contribute meaningfully to our community.

In essence, the collaboration of these puzzle pieces transform our comfort zone from a confined space into a launchpad for expansive growth and a vibrant, purpose-driven life.

A TRANSFORMATIVE JOURNEY

Mastering these seven pillars is what propelled me to the next level in my life, career, ministry, family, and community. Embarking on a journey beyond your comfort zone is a profound endeavor that requires a strategic approach. Let's consider the significance of mastering these seven pillars that include prayer, passion, purpose, potential, persistence, preparation, and a positive mindset—as you aim to achieve your goals.

1. **Prayer:** Commencing your journey with prayer establishes a strong foundation. It provides a sense of guidance and spiritual support, fostering a connection with your inner self and the power of God. Prayer can instill peace and clarity, serving as a source of strength as you navigate uncharted territories.
2. **Passion:** Passion is the driving force that propels you forward. When you are fueled by passion, challenges become opportunities, and obstacles transform into stepping stones. It ignites the fire within, motivating you to persevere and excel in the pursuit of your goals.
3. **Purpose:** Clarifying your purpose aligns your actions with a greater meaning. Understanding why you're stepping

beyond your comfort zone gives direction to your efforts. It serves as a compass, guiding you through uncertainties and reinforcing your commitment to personal and professional growth.

4. **Potential:** Recognizing and unlocking your potential is pivotal. Each step outside your comfort zone unveils new facets of your possibilities. Embrace the belief that you have untapped greatness within you. Cultivate a mindset that sees challenges as opportunities to discover and harness your full potential.

5. **Persistence:** Persistence is the cornerstone of resilience. The journey beyond your comfort zone is bound to present challenges, but persistence ensures that setbacks are viewed as temporary roadblocks rather than insurmountable barriers. It fuels the determination needed to navigate difficulties and continue moving forward.

6. **Preparation:** Thorough preparation is essential for success. Equip yourself with the knowledge, skills, and resources necessary for the challenges that lie ahead. Preparation builds confidence, enabling you to face uncertainties with a sense of readiness and assurance.

7. **Positive Mindset:** Maintaining a positive mindset is transformative. It shapes your perception of challenges, fostering a mindset that views setbacks as opportunities for growth. Positivity enables you to overcome self-doubt and fear, empowering you to embrace change with optimism and resilience.

Since I began mastering these seven pillars, it created a holistic framework for stepping beyond my comfort zone. As you integrate prayer, passion, purpose, potential, persistence, preparation, and a positive mindset into your journey, you cultivate a powerful mindset that propels you toward the achievement of your goals. Remember, you have greatness inside of you that people are waiting to experience—embrace the journey with enthusiasm, reflection, and actionable steps. As we embrace these seven pillars, let's remember: Transformation isn't an event; it's a process. And that process can begin right now in your life, in this very moment.

As I conclude, the transition into the upcoming significant moments in life proves to be highly gratifying. The journey is real, and it resonates with the authenticity of embracing discomfort for the sake of growth. The exploration of seven transformative benefits to stepping beyond our comfort zone sets the stage, revealing a path to personal growth, increased resilience, expanded creativity, enhanced confidence, improved decision-making, broadened perspectives, and the triumphant achievement of goals. Yet, as some of my story evolves, it becomes evident that life is not a singular thread but a tapestry woven from intricate puzzle pieces. These pieces, represented by God, family, career, finances, health, personal and professional development, community, and lifelong learning, intricately interlock, forming the essence of our existence. This narrative invites us to be real, to confront the challenges and joys that come with stepping beyond comfort zones, assembling the puzzle pieces that together paint a portrait of a transformative journey toward depth, purpose, and continual exploration.

The writing unfolds as a genuine exploration of life's complexities and the rewards that lie beyond the familiar, urging us to embrace discomfort and propel toward pivotal moments of self-discovery and fulfillment.

DR. VALARIE W. HARRIS

Dr. Valarie W. Harris, with more than forty years of experience in education, has dedicated her life to empowering young adults, educators, women leaders, and entrepreneurs on a global scale, always emphasizing the importance of aligning passion with purpose and building legacies for future generations.

Dr. Valarie's academic journey has been rich, with degrees from Norfolk State University, Virginia Tech University, and Seraphim Ministries International Bible College, complemented by her worship studies degree from Liberty University and a doctoral degree from Seraphim Ministries International Bible College. Her global commitment extends to various locations, including Ghana, India, Alaska, Puerto Rico, Amsterdam, London, Brussels, Paris, and the Caribbean, with a special focus on humanitarian efforts in Grenada.

As the founder of Stepping Out with Purpose, LLC Coaching & Consulting Company, Dr. Valarie's mission revolves around empowering individuals to craft businesses that go beyond financial success and resonate through generations. Her role as an educator, minister, empowerment coach, business consultant, and author, with nine books under her belt and her collaborations, highlights her commitment to personal growth and empowerment.

In her heart, Dr. Valarie strives to be a beacon of wisdom and empowerment in the realms of education, leadership, and personal growth, guiding others toward their fullest potential and unique journeys. Through her legacy, she aims to ignite empowerment that transcends generations and transforms the landscape of education and leadership.

TRUSTING GOD'S PLAN
REVEREND SONYA M. MATTHEWS

"For I know the plans I have for you," declares the Lord, *"plans to prosper you and not to harm you, plans to give you hope and a future.*
—Jeremiah 29:11 (NIV)

T rust is a very fragile thing.

- We trust that when we sit in a chair, it will support our weight.
- We trust the car will start when we push the bottom or turn the key.
- We trust our family and friends to love and support us.
- We trust our employer to provide a safe environment for us to work in.
- We trust society to be fair and open-minded.

However, when we place our trust in the hands of people and things, it can easily be bruised, broken, misused, violated, and even destroyed. Once trust has been damaged, it is very hard to step into another situation that requires us to trust again, which makes it more difficult for the next person or thing that comes along with good intentions. That is why trusting the plan(s) of God may be a bit more difficult than most of us really want to admit. Trusting God means believing in His reliability, His Word, His ability, and His strength. Trusting God will make everything alright.

Our natural man wants to have his own way and do his own things, which sometimes lands us between a rock and a hard place. We know how determined we can be when it comes to having our own way, which can lead to making the same mistakes, running into the same brick wall(s), tripping over our own feet, maneuvering ourselves into a corner, and repeating the same behaviors over and over and over again, which ends up with the same unsuccessful results. However, I must be fair: There are certainly times we face predicaments through no fault of our own. Trusting God's plans does not mean we will live a life without challenges, hardships, loss, or difficulties; however, we would be aligned with the one who is the answer and has the answers for every past, present, and future situation.

For many of us, if we are completely honest, truly trusting God's plan comes when there is no other option or we have exhausted every option available to us, and we desperately need Him to intervene when God's desire is that we walk by faith and not by sight. He wants us to totally trust and depend on Him.

So, why do we willingly settle for less when God has a better way—the ultimate plan—and a specific purpose for each of us? He is the one who created us in Him own image. God has anointed us, appointed us, called us, empowered us, equipped us, and gifted us to be all that He created us to be. God's plans for us were completed before we arrived on the scene. Jeremiah 1:5 (NLT) reminds us, *"I knew you before I formed you in your mother's womb. Before you were born I set you apart and appointed you as my prophet to the nations."*

When we are willing to allow God to take control and trust His plan for our life, ready or not, change will come.

Merriam-Webster defines change as *to make (someone or something) different; alter or modify.* As a noun, it is *the act or instance of making or becoming different.*

According to my research, traditionally there are seven components to trusting.

1. **Integrity**—securely believing in someone to make good-faith agreements, tell the truth, and fulfill their promises.
2. **Competence**—the aspect of trust when we view someone as having the correct knowledge, skill, ability, and competency in a given situation.
3. **Consistency**—always behaving in the same way and having the same attitude toward people or things or to achieve the same level of success in something.
4. **Credibility**—the quality of being trustworthy or believable.
5. **Ability**—possessing the skills to do something or enabling a person to have influence within a specific domain.
6. **Honesty**—the fairness and straightforwardness of conduct and being free from deceit.
7. **Compassion**—to suffer with someone or acting to alleviate the suffering of others.

I think it is important to mention that these components of trust are all attributes of God.

Even though you may not know:

- What God's plan is, please recognize we are not always given the details or the information we feel is necessary ("*For* as *the heavens are higher than the earth, So are My ways higher than your ways, And My thoughts than your thoughts"* Isaiah 55:9 NKJV).

- When the plan will unfold...just know God is doing it *(Being confident of this very thing, that He which hath begun a good work in you will perform it until the day of Jesus Christ"* Philippians 1:6 KJV).

- Where will the plan take you, understanding that your steps have been ordered by God (*"The steps of a good man are ordered by the LORD, And He delights in his way. Though he fall, he shall not be utterly cast down; For the LORD upholds him with His hand"* Psalm 37: 23–24 NIV).

- Why did He choose you for the assignment? It is your destiny (*"And those He predestined, He also called; those He called, He also justified; those He justified, He also glorified"* Romans 8:30 NKJV).

- How will you carry out His plan? Just know that God is well able to lead you and guide you (*"Trust in the LORD with all your heart, And lean not on your own understanding; In all your ways acknowledge Him, And He shall direct your paths"* Proverb 3:5–6 NKJV).

History paints a clear picture of what happens when change takes place. Over the years, as a people and as a society, we have seen changes bring out the worst in folks, even when it is for their good; however, changing can also bring out the best in us. After being in the workforce for forty years, it appears to me that most people don't necessarily mind change (because even the seasons change), but they just don't want to *be* changed.

Transitioning—the process or a period of changing from one state or condition to another—from our way to God's way may not be easy and may even be painful, but it is necessary. Whenever God begins to shift us into the new place that holds His plan and purpose, our lives will never be the same.

What is our responsibility in trusting God? We must be determined to build a relationship that fosters developing trust in Him. It is just like in a relationship with people—you want to develop or strengthen a relationship with someone who interests you. You spend time with that person to find out:

- Whether you are compatible.
- What they expect out of the relationship and how or if that matches what you need and want.
- About their character—who they say they are, and are they accountable for what they say they will do?
- Can you count on them during the good, the bad, and the ugly?
- Are they honest, faithful, and responsible?
- What are their likes and dislikes? Can you live with that list?
- Do they have dreams, desire, hopes, goals, vision, and a plan on how to get there?
- How do their dreams, desires, hopes, goals, vision, and plans fit with where you see yourself going?
- Are you willing to support this?
- Are they willing to respect you and support your dreams, desires, hopes, goals, and vision?

When you trust God's plan, you will begin to understand why you were created and what He has placed deep down inside of you. As you now walk by faith in God, depending on the one who is able to keep you from falling, your possibilities and your capabilities become endless. Trusting God's plan will give you peace and fill your heart with joy. He has strategically orchestrated every moment from your beginning until your time has ended. His plan was customized specifically with you in mind. His plan will connect you to your true purpose, and He will give you the strength you need to endure.

I recently found myself in a situation where I literally had no other option but to trust the plans of God. Not to say that I am disobedient on a regular basis, but I am human. I was led to become a mission team member of Uniquely Chosen Ministries, traveling to Ghana, West Africa in May 2023. I was humbled and excited to be part of such an extraordinary opportunity.

During the preparation for this trip, my father's health began to decline, but since God was leading me to go to Ghana, I prayed and had faith, without a shadow of a doubt that God would keep my dad until I returned. Two days before the team flew out (Saturday), I told my dad I was going away for a short time and expected him to be there when I got back. As usual, I kissed him on his forehead, then leaned in so he could kiss me on my cheek, and told him I would see him soon and I loved him.

After a few minor obstacles, by the grace of God, we arrived safely to our first hotel destination in Ghana. That was late Tuesday. Now the real journey began as the mission team embarked on God's plan being revealed.

On Wednesday, we were out in the community servicing and being blessed by this wonderful experience and the remarkable people. But, on our way back to the hotel, after our final service for the evening, my phone rang. It was my cousin calling to say my dad was failing, and hospice wanted to step in. I literally felt like I was being punked. I could hardly believe what I was hearing. After all, I did ask God to keep my dad until I returned home, and I know God hears me when I pray. So, at that point, I thanked my cousin Valerie for all she had done as my surrogate while I was away, but told her from this point on, hospice would need to speak directly to me before they did anything. I needed specific details, and I had questions and concerns. Valerie understood and went on to say that hospice wanted to start their intervention on Friday when his assigned nurse returned. I asked her to leave a message for the hospice nurse to contact me, and I would do the same.

Thank God for the amazing women He purposed to be a part of the mission team. When I told them about my phone conversation, they *immediately* rallied around me, wrapped their arms around me, physically held me up, covering me in prayer, encouraged me, and reminded me to breathe. To God be the glory for them all.

God's plan moved forward. On Thursday, May 18, 2023, when my cell phone rang around 4:30 a.m. (Ghana is four hours ahead of Virginia), it was my cousin breaking the news that my dad had passed. I had been my dad's caregiver and power of attorney for more than ten years. It felt like I had been hit with a ton of bricks. It was like something inside of me had died too. I don't really remember our entire conversation. I just remember shouting, "WHAT?"

At that point, I had no answers, just questions that no one could answer except God. I remember feeling numb as I walked next door to share the news about my dad with the mission team leader, Reverend Pamela H. McLaughlin. When someone knocks on your door that early in the morning, it is usually not good news. I remember getting the words out about my dad, but saying it added to the numbness I already felt. Reverend McLaughlin and I talked, and before leaving her room, she told me she would check on getting me home.

I went back to my room and had a conversation with God: *I cannot believe you took my dad while I'm here on the mission field serving your people. I asked you to keep my dad until I returned home. I thought you sent me here, but I must have heard you wrong. I am not supposed to be here,* then I began to cry uncontrollably.

If I had known May 13, 2023, was the last time I would see my dad; the last time I would kiss him and he'd kiss me; the very last time I would be able to look into his eyes and say I love you, would I have done anything different? Would I have traveled more than eight thousand miles for the experience of a lifetime? I never imagined that one of the highest moments in life would be coupled with the very lowest moment of my life, but God had a plan, and my job was to trust Him.

After I finally stopped crying, I could feel God embracing me. He said, *Yes, I sent you to Ghana, but I called your dad home.* And I heard my dad say, "I have lived my life, now you live yours and finish your assignment." What could I say to the God who is the author and finisher of our faith (Hebrews 12:2), also knowing that my dad *always* supported me in ministry. I cleaned myself up and got dressed, collected my gear for the day, then stopped back by Reverend McLaughlin's room to give her my decision. I told her about my encounter and that I would be staying to finish the assignment. She appeared surprised—I was surprised too—but I knew staying was what I was supposed to do, and I prayed my children would be okay with my decision.

I made my way to breakfast, and I was sitting there counting the minutes before I would call Justin and Shayla. Shortly after this, the other members of the mission team found out about my situation and immediately began to provide support for me. I am so grateful for each of them. I stepped away to call my son with the news about Pop Pop. The conversation ended with Justin telling me, "Mom, you need to stay focused so you can finish your assignment."

I later spoke with my daughter, and she responded with, "Mom, are you okay, because you have to stay."

I could not believe what I had heard. My first thought was, *Who are these children that understand the gravity of why I came to Ghana and know I have to stay and finish the work?* That was a powerful moment for me as they confirmed what I already knew. I dedicate this chapter to Justin G. Matthews and Shayla N. Matthews for understanding the cost of trusting God's plan as they selflessly encouraged me to stay in the midst of our loss and grief. I love you.

As the mission trip continued, even through the moments of pain, I knew I was in the right place and God had called me to serve in this capacity. Imagine planning a homegoing service while on the mission field, but God gave me the strength and support I needed to carry out the plans He had for me. Every provision was in place—all I had to do was ask. The outpouring of love, support, and assistance even from across the waters was amazing. I experienced a different kind of love I had never experienced before. It was God's love demonstrated on earth, and it was humbling. No one has to walk through the midst of a heartache and sorrow without the strength of God, for His grace was surely sufficient for me. God had already established a plan, and all I had to do was put my trust in Him. Even when I was too weary to trace Him, I could walk in faith because I could trust Him.

When you walk in a place of trusting God's plan, the transformation will be significant. In these moments, I did not even recognize myself, as God was doing a work in me.

Serving God and trusting His plan comes with a cost. Please know that everyone will not be happy as you move forward to become who God called and created you to be. They won't understand your walk because they cannot fit your shoes.

People who know you may not understand the ways you now move because they don't hear what you hear. Some people will have an opinion that may not be kind, but who are they to judge you? As we trust God's plan and He does a new thing in our lives, some individuals will not survive the shift, but that's alright. He will bring the people into your life who are supposed to be there as He removes the ones whose time is up. You will experience a newness that you have never experienced before, and it can be lonely as He moves you from one plan to another.

Throughout this chapter, I have mentioned benefits of trusting God's plan, for they far outweigh every cost. Here are just a few more to consider: Trusting God's plan will also give you faith in His promises, hope for your future, and a new perspective.

My hope is that you will be encouraged to trust the plans of the One who promised never to leave us or forsake us. He is the beginning of all things and is where everything will end. He is the one with a perfect plan and worthy of us placing our trust in Him. If you are interested in finding out more about the One who has proven Himself since the test of time, I recommend you read and study His Word, the Bible. It is the number one bestseller of all time. God bless you in your pursuit to trusting His plan.

REVEREND SONYA M. MATTHEWS

Reverend Sonya M. Matthews is an esteemed authority in behavioral health administration, leadership, and training others. She has embarked on a compelling journey that intertwines academic prowess, spiritual leadership, and a profound commitment to community service.

Armed with a bachelor of science in organizational leadership and management, Sonya seamlessly applies her academic acumen in her impactful role at the Veterans Health Administration, where she brings a wealth of expertise to the realm of behavioral health administration. Her dedication to fostering well-being and empowerment is not only evident in her professional pursuits but also in her long-standing service at Mt. Olivet Baptist Church for more than twenty-five years, where she has also served as a licensed associate minister since December 2016.

As a trailblazer in prayer, Sonya serves as the co-facilitator of the women's intercessory prayer ministry, extending her influence globally as a mission team member of Uniquely Chosen Ministries in Africa 2023. Her ability to navigate diverse settings and make a meaningful impact showcases a leadership style that transcends boundaries.

She is a servant and a worshipper. In her pursuit of knowledge and spiritual growth, Sonya is an active student of the School of the Prophets.

Sonya's heartfelt desire extends beyond herself; it's a commitment to the betterment of humanity. As a mother, she weaves her passion into her family life, aiming not only to see individuals saved, delivered, healed, and set free, but also to instill these values in her children, Justin and Shayla.

One of the scriptures she stands on is 1 John 5:14–15, *"And this is the confidence that we have in him, that, if we ask any thing according to his will, he heareth us: And if we know that he hears us, whatsoever we ask, we know that we have the petitions that we desired of him."*

WE CAN DO HARD THINGS
SHYRELLE J. SCOTT

My mom always used to tell me, "The Lord never gives you more than you can handle."

I can't help but ponder on that phrase, and sometimes more than not, I question if that was actually true. I can honestly say I have been through many ups and downs, life-changing struggles, but nothing I think could have ever prepared me for what I was about to experience.

One would say I have lived a pretty privileged life. I grew up in a two-parent household, and my father worked while my mom stayed home with my brother and me. I have so many wonderful memories of growing up in my community. I had lots of friends, and we would hang out and play until the street light came on, which signaled us that it was time to retreat home and have dinner with the family. We would always have dinner around the table and discuss the day. That was the best part of the day for me because I had both my mom and my dad's undivided attention as we discussed the happenings of school.

We would have dinner, and my dad would be off to do his night hustle, which was playing at a local club at an army base. My dad had many talents, one being an extraordinary musician. He could compose songs and play multiple instruments. I loved hearing him sing the many songs he spent many late nights working on. The music brought him so much joy.

My mom would be a fixture in the room as he wrote and played songs. She was his biggest fan and supporter in everything that he did. I marveled at how my mom would look at my dad and how he would reciprocate that back at her. I would always tell myself that one day I'd have what they had. It truly was special, and it resonated with both me and my brother almost fifty years later. My brother played baseball and football and was in the Cub Scouts, while I spent most of my childhood years in dance.

Although the holidays were a big thing in our house, we didn't necessarily have to have something special happening to get together. We had big families on both sides, so we always had family over for cookouts or just hanging out playing cards and eating the yummy food that everyone would bring. Both of our grannies were amazing cooks, especially my Grandma Jones. She would make desserts from scratch that would make your mouth salivate with anticipation of sampling her delectable delights. You could taste the love in her food. Thanksgiving would be a mass production. Lots of prep for the meal the night before in the kitchen with my mom and aunt listening to the music, laughing, having a great old time. Nothing beats those moments. I looked forward to those moments year after year.

Even as a wife and mother, going to my mom's Thanksgiving Eve was the tradition, and I stuck to it. Christmas was such a magical time for us. However, I must say I think Mom and Dad loved it even more than my brother and I did. They had that extra twinkle in their eye during this time of year.

Traditionally, on a weeknight, at the start of the season, my family would ride to Richmond to the mall, and our parents would let us go from store to store showing all the things we liked. We would also visit Santa and tell him everything we wanted. Then on to the toy store where we could also pick our wish-list items. We would eat out at a fancy restaurant, laughing, having just the best time with my perfect little family, pure joy just oozing from our pores; we just loved every second of it all. Decorating the Christmas tree and decking the halls with beautiful ornaments making the house look festive, while Luther Vandross' and The Temptations' Christmas music played in the background. Christmas morning, we would wake up and see mostly all of our things we picked out under the tree. Mom and Dad would beam with delight as we spent our morning ravishing through the many beautifully wrapped gifts.

I could go on and on about the many memories I had growing up. I feel it's imperative that I preface my childhood in order for one to understand the depth of love, joy, and happiness that is the cornerstone of who I am. As I've grown into the woman I am today, I often look back at my childhood and think there was nothing extraordinary about it. I always thought everyone's family was like mine, but I couldn't be more wrong.

I've had family members, friends of the family, even coworkers of my dad tell me, "You and your brother were blessed."

Yes, I knew we were blessed because our parents instilled in us the importance of family and taught us many of the lessons of life such as honor and respect for others as well as yourself. More importantly, Mom took me and my brother to church almost every Sunday. In my mind, those were practices that all families participated in. I realize now that what I experienced was not a norm, but an extreme rarity.

As I've grown into the woman I am today—married with my own children—I've tried to instill, replicate, and continue some of the same teachings with my own family. The many traditions I loved so much as a child growing up, I wanted my kids to have the same memories, the same feelings, but I've learned that some things don't always work out as planned. I can say that we have shared and experienced a lot of the same traditions, but we also have started some of our own. Being an educator has afforded me opportunities to have special times with my children, and I'm grateful for that. My children also have been blessed with the gift of having my mom and dad as grandparents and experiencing life with them.

I believe the best gift I could have ever given my parents was making them grandparents. Family and friends have told me I was spoiled; well, my kids are rotten! I don't believe my parents used the word *no* for either of my children about anything, but I was okay with it. I am thankful for it.

Fast forward to the summer of 2021. In this instance, I must say that God knew just how much I could handle. In May of that year, I had graduated with my master's in education, and we had a small celebration with family and friends for this milestone. My parents couldn't be prouder of me during that time. Covid was not as rampant, and my dad was still very cautious about being around large crowds, but he came to the gathering because he wanted to celebrate me. My mom was also there, but she hadn't been herself lately. She had complained some about minor stomach pain and not having much of an appetite. I also noticed she had lost a few pounds because she wasn't eating. However, she didn't let any of it get her down.

Early June, school had been out for the summer for just a few days, and my dad called to say he was taking mom to the emergency room. She was having major pains in her stomach. I immediately knew that wasn't good. Mom never complained. He said he would call when he knew more. A couple hours later, he called and asked me to come to the hospital; they'd found a spot on an X-ray.

As I was driving there, I couldn't help but think the worst. However, I was praying the entire way that it can be fixed—healed. As I walked in, I saw my mom, and I looked into her eyes and saw they were filled with tears and fear. I'd never seen my mom in this way.

I just held her and said to her, "It's going to be okay, Mom, no matter what."

As I held her, I looked over at my dad, and he looked at me with hopelessness, fear in his eyes—a look I'd never seen before—and it scared me. As my brother and I waited in silence in the emergency room, we both looked at each other lost and confused.

What was about to happen? Were we going to lose the core of our family? Our rock?

Dad came out and told us that Mom had pancreatic cancer. For a moment, it felt like my world had just stopped. How was this possible? She was the healthiest person I knew. I may have seen her fight the flu once in my fifty years of life. I was stunned. I couldn't even cry. All I wanted to do at that moment was see her. That night was the beginning of a journey that I never thought I would be on, especially not with my mom, my best friend, my person.

I am thankful to God that He kept this until after I had finished the year of school because I wouldn't have been able to handle such news and work. The next few months were stressful, yet blessings because I was given one more day to spend with Mom who endured chemotherapy for several months. It wasn't easy for her small, petite frame, but she was a trouper, a warrior. She never complained, continued to go about her days as normal as she could until she just couldn't any longer.

During this time, I celebrated my milestone birthday—my fiftieth—and Mom, her seventieth. We celebrated Mom's birthday in the hospital as she was having some issues with her cancer. During her stay in the hospital, we also learned the devastating news that there was nothing else that could be done for her. While we were all surrounding her bed while the doctor was talking to us, tears were flowing like a river down my cheeks.

All the while, my momma was wiping away my tears and smiling at me. "It's gonna be alright, punkin. Trust God."

We left the hospital with my mom going into hospice care. Her wish was to be home with her family, and that is what we did. The next few weeks were tough—nothing like I've ever experienced. I was given the gift of being with Mom on her last days on this earth. I was able to take care of her as she once took care of me so many years ago. We had moments of laughter, tears, and sometimes silence.

Some things just didn't need to be said; they were understood. Family came by to have their moments with Mom, saying their goodbyes. It was a very solemn, dark time; however, Mom always managed to hold a conversation and show that beautiful, infectious smile of hers to her family and friends just one more time. What I remember so vividly from that time were the moments she had with her two grandchildren and my dad. The kids would be in the bed with her, and she would talk and have a few laughs with them. You could see the tiredness in her eyes, but she stayed alert enough to tell them how much they were loved by her. Daddy barely slept those three weeks. He never left her side unless she had visitors. I basically camped out at the house, only leaving to check on my own family at home, shower, and back again. One day, my mom and I had "the conversation," the talk no one ever wants to have, and I definitely wasn't prepared for it.

However, the love I had for her and my strong desire and commitment to her happiness in her last moments carried me through. From her clothing she wanted to wear, to whether she wanted to wear a wig was all discussed that day. I cried through it all like a baby, and as always she comforted me, reassuring me that I was strong and could handle what was coming next.

She was preparing me in her own way to handle the duties of being the caregiver of the family—not only my dad and brother but her siblings and everyone else who would feel the loss that would soon be coming.

I was not ready. How could God do this? How could he take away my constant, my best friend, my biggest cheerleader in life, my momma? I couldn't make sense of it. Mom's body was getting weaker by the day. At this point, she was not really eating or drinking. Hospice nurses warned us that this would happen and not to force it.

Apparently, our bodies naturally shut down, and these are just steps through that process. Mom sat and wrote all of us letters. It took several days and many breaks in between due to fatigue, but she was determined to finish, and she did. She wrote them and sealed them with a kiss in envelopes with directions for us not to open them until she was gone.

My brother and I would take turns walking my mom around the house because that was all she had the energy for, and as we walked, she would lift her hands up in the air praising God for all He had done. She whispered, "Thank you, Father. You've been so good." She praised Him until she physically could not speak.

I will forever remember the moments I washed her face, bathed her, sprayed her perfume. I would whisper softly in her ear that I loved her. She would squeeze my hand, or she would move her eyes acknowledging my voice. When Mommy took her last breath on that Thursday evening, we were all there at her bedside just as she wanted. I felt numb. The pain and sorrow were so overwhelming I felt like I couldn't breathe. My sweet mom was gone.

After we laid my mom to rest, I wasn't truly able to mourn because my focus was now on my dad and making sure he was okay. He had his own health issues, which he chose to ignore while dealing with my mom's diagnosis. Daddy is diabetic, and he's had circulation issues for many years, even had a couple toes amputated. He had been putting off getting help for his circulation issues because as always, he had to take care of mom—"fix mom" like he was able to do most of our lives, fix things. However, he couldn't fix it, and it changed him. He was no longer the dad we had always known.

I remember talking to my dad just a couple days before my mom passed. We were on the deck, taking in some sun and fresh air. I looked at Dad and said, "I can't lose both you and Mom. I couldn't handle that."

"I won't leave y'all," he said. "Your mother and I talked, and I'm going to be here for us all. I won't leave you, punkin."

Over the next few months, after going from doctor to doctor, we had come to the conclusion that Dad would need to have a below-knee amputation. He struggled with not just the thought of having part of his limb amputated, but the thoughts of how life would be for him and how it would affect me and my brother. My dad never wanted to be a burden to anyone; he was the most independent man I have ever known. Although we had many talks about how life could still be full and productive and after rehab, how he could still drive and do things he usually did, he still had doubts. However, he never verbalized them. He continued to remain as positive and optimistic as he could.

Late August, my father had the surgery and came through with flying colors. He was definitely having pain, but we were able to manage it, and after a week of recovering in the hospital, he was then transported to a rehabilitation hospital where he would begin the next chapter in his life, trying to adjust to a new way of living. It was not easy, and from the very beginning, I could see a change in my dad's spirit. He wasn't the talkative, jovial guy who would hold a conversation with you. He was quite withdrawn—you had to start a conversation with him, otherwise he didn't talk much.

I was visiting daily, watching him go to his rehab sessions, and his head was always low. He gave very little effort in what the therapists were asking him to do. I could feel him getting more and more withdrawn. Each day, I came with the intent to put a smile on his face and provide encouraging words, letting him know how well he was doing and to not give up. After a couple weeks of being there, he was sent back to the hospital because he had a small infection that the rehab hospital couldn't address—nothing life threatening, but he needed medical attention. While at the hospital, my dad still wasn't eating like he should or drinking. He appeared to me more depressed each day.

However, this one afternoon I was visiting Dad, and we had a good visit. We talked, even had a few laughs. As usual, he told me to get out of there and get home to my family before it got too late. I told him to make sure he ate his dinner because he needed to build up his strength so he could get out of there. He smiled at me and said, "I'll try."

The next morning while just getting settled in at work, I got a call from his doctor saying they were giving him CPR; they found him nonresponsive on their morning rounds. It was God's grace that guided me to the hospital that morning. My heart was beating outside of my chest; the thought of my dad no longer with us had taken over. As I arrived on the floor, a group of doctors were standing outside my dad's room. At that moment, I knew my daddy was gone. As I walked in the room and saw his lifeless body lying there, I couldn't help but think, *I am alone now. I have no one, the two most important people in my life are now gone.* As I sat next to him holding his hand and tears running down my face, I could hear a voice telling me, *He is okay. He is with his soulmate.*

My daddy was a changed man after Mom died. He stopped playing his music, he stopped doing anything that brought him joy. A huge part of my dad perished the day Mom died. He gave it all he had to be here with us, but he knew he had to join her. Within six months, I lost my world. Although I had a husband and children, losing not just one parent, but both within months of each other is almost unimaginable, at times cruel.

After laying my dear father to rest, the thought of him now reunited with Mom gave me some peace, but I was still so very empty and often felt alone in this big, unpredictable, scary world we live in. Getting up to start a new day was so exhausting. There were days where I didn't want to get up out of bed—days where I screamed and cried for them both, sometimes angry at God for taking them away because I still had so much I wanted to do with them or share with them. I wanted them to see my youngest graduate high school and start college. I wanted them to see my children marry and start families of their own.

Yet, I had to understand that it wasn't God's plan. It has now been a year and half since this journey started, and I find myself still asking questions and wondering why this happened to me, but what has carried me through this process is my strong faith in God. What these losses have taught me or are still teaching me is that God is real and that He will take care of you. So many times I've felt like giving up, but God! Through God's grace and mercy, I have been able to step outside of my comfort zone and experience those hard moments I had to go through in caring for my mom then caring for my dad. Most days started with a big cry, but I realized I was needed, and I pulled it together and pushed forward.

Now I focus on being here for my children and being the best parent I can be for them. If I can be half the parent mine were to me, I'm doing something right. Most importantly, I do not want the legacy of my parents to be tarnished or forgotten. Their one goal in life was to ensure that they raised kind, God-fearing humans and to provide them with life experiences that will help them grow into productive citizens of society. I'd like to think that they did accomplish that.

Their teachings and unconditional love exudes within me, and I try daily to pass that along, not only to my children, but to anyone I may come in contact with along my journey in life.

I have truly been pushed, challenged beyond my limits. I never would have thought that little old me would have had the strength, courage, the guts to take on the job of caring for my parents, but as I think back and reflect on the daunting tasks I had to endure, I would not change one thing. I could never repay my loving parents for everything they ever did for me, my brother, and my family.

I would like to dedicate this chapter to my wonderful mom and dad, Larry and Shirley Jones. I am the person I am because of their guidance, patience, and love. I hope that they know that we miss them immensely and feel their absence each and every day, but we all put one foot in front of the other and move forward through life because we know that is what they expect from us all. Every morning I look up at the horizon—the beautiful creation God makes every day —and I smile because I know the sun shines brighter, more extraordinarily beautiful because my parents are smiling down, and I feel their presence beaming down upon me. Each passing day, I wake up with a new sense of hope and anticipation that God will not give me more than I can handle. All I need to do is trust his plan, and I will be alright.

One of my favorite Bible verses that I reference daily is from Joshua 1:9, *"Have I not commanded you? Be strong and courageous. Do not be afraid; do not be discouraged, for the Lord your God will be with you wherever you go."*

For those who may have experienced or are going through a loss, let this be a testament that you can make it, and you will be able to live life as God would want you to. Be encouraged.

SHYRELLE J. SCOTT

Shyrelle J. Scott, an esteemed educator of two decades, began her journey as a dedicated English teacher in Petersburg, Virginia, later expanding her impact to Richmond and Powhatan County. Currently serving as the literacy coach at Powhatan Middle School, she's deeply passionate about helping young minds achieve their goals and nurturing a profound love for reading and literacy. Shyrelle firmly believes that literacy is the key to empowerment, self-reliance, and civic engagement. In her role, she supports students and colleagues alike, offering resources, mentorship, and professional development to address the needs of students with reading challenges.

Shyrelle's love for reading originated in her childhood, a cherished gift from her mother. Her academic journey led her from Petersburg High School to a bachelor of arts in English from Virginia State University and a master of science in education with a reading concentration from Old Dominion University. She's a perpetual learner, advocating that it's never too late to find one's passion and purpose in life.

Throughout her distinguished career, Shyrelle has donned various roles, including membership in the principal's advisory board, school newspaper editor, student council association sponsor, new teacher mentor, school leadership team member, spelling bee coordinator, and junior beta club sponsor.

Beyond her professional life, Shyrelle's personal mission is to be a blessing to those around her, exemplifying the importance of kindness and paying it forward. These values, instilled by her parents from a young age, remain a guiding force in her life.

Shyrelle shares her life's journey with her husband, William, who is also an educator, and their two children.

GROW IN CHARACTER, INTEGRITY, GRIT, GRIND, AND GRACE

TISHA L. SKINNER

Most people would like to say that their career paths were clear with every step already mapped out, but the truth is, most of us experience this thing called *Life*. I like to view life as the things we have no control over and the things that we do, all at the same time. Either way, life is a gift. If many of us looked back over our lives five, ten, fifteen years ago, we likely had no idea we would end up where we are now. The older and wiser we become, the more we value time, the more we understand that LIFE continually evolves, and the more we accept that we must evolve with it.

To evolve is to not only to change but to grow from one state to another. No matter how well we plan or how much education we receive, a career path is a journey. Our paths evolve over struggle, over sacrifice, over joy, over determination, over tears, over desire, and over time. Development is truly a process in and out of season. As we grow to respect the process, we learn that every failure brings new opportunities. We eventually see that all things work together for the good of those who love the Lord.

As I examine my life from a young child to adulthood, there are five things that have contributed to various successes in my career journey. Character, integrity, grit, grind, and grace are all attributes that have shaped my personal and professional development.

I think it is important to share the beginnings of my story. I grew up in a seaside resort town with a small population of people of color. Most resided in my immediate neighborhood, and a few families scattered across the western part of town. Typically, people of color resided there as decedents of many generations who settled from years past.

My community was small but close-knit. It was a time when neighbors were like family, and you could borrow a cup of sugar. However, outside the comfort of my neighborhood, the reality of racial disparity was alive and well. As a young child, it was understood what restaurants and business establishments not to enter, which beaches not to enter, and which parts of town not to frequent.

I was usually the only child of color in a classroom and part of a school system with no full-time teachers of color during my entire K–12 experience. My graduation class had approximately 268 students, ten of whom were people of color. I grew up as a young girl with different clothes, different hair, different foods, different music, and an altogether different culture. Those differences created a huge internal struggle with the rest of the world in learning to balance the value of race, ethnicity, and understanding of my authentic self. I was forced to learn identify, self-worth, and walk in my truth, simply as a form of psychological survival, much earlier than any child should. I was called a nigger and jungle bunny before age eight, and I've seen the Ku Klux Klan walk through my neighborhood as my 4-H camp counselor kept us quiet in the basement of our church. This was not in the 1930s or 1940s in the Deep South, this was the late 1970s and 1980s in the so-called progressive North.

Much of what I experienced growing up did not fully resonate until I attended a historically black university. Ironically, stepping onto the campus from a place of discomfort to a new comfort zone was still somewhat uncomfortable. You see, the normal I had known all my life was never actually normal. On campus, much of me felt a newfound peace and acceptance, while totally operating outside my comfort zone.

I entered undergrad determined to change the world through the study of political science and prelaw. My interest in the criminal justice system is connected to what I witnessed as a child.

For many years, a dear childhood friend would suffer repeated acts of violence, as she, her baby sister, and her two brothers would witness a continual cycle of their father assaulting their mother. Her family members, friends, neighbors, and people within our small community would witness and have knowledge of the violence, yet rarely would get involved or intervene. Despite our close-knit community, certain things like domestic violence were not openly discussed. Everyone minded their own business.

Her mother eventually gained the courage and support to escape the violence and relocate to another state with her baby sister. My friend settled with family members. Her brothers remained with the father for many years thereafter. My friend was one of the smartest, most resilient people I have ever known. Although I never experienced any level of violence in my childhood or adult family homes, to experience the secondary trauma alongside my friend completely changed how I viewed people, the value of life, and how the world responds. I wanted to understand human behavior and why people hurt people. I knew I wanted to change systems and to help those who hurt. As a young child, I was fascinated with the criminal justice system, the order of law, and what caused people to make certain choices.

GROW IN CHARACTER

Character—the mental, moral qualities distinctive to a person

I started my career as a young woman in graduate school and moved to a management level position in a little under five years. Again, outside of my comfort zone, I interviewed along with three unknown senior staff members, older in age with longer experience in the field, at an unfamiliar agency in another county.

I submitted my application fifteen minutes before the deadline as I had no expectation of receiving the position. I applied, fully trusting God to open the door if it was for me or to close the door if it was not. My boss confirmed I received the position because I was able to present with purpose and vision, despite the other candidates having lengthier backgrounds. You see, they designed the position to develop the first specialized domestic violence local probation unit in the state, and it required someone with fresh perspective, somewhat fearless, and able to build partnerships. Little did I know or fully understand the depth of my potential and what I was stepping into.

In serving as a supervisor for over half of my career, I would say the greatest challenge was learning how to adequately assess personalities. Later, I understood that every person reflects their upbringing, life experiences, thoughts, and belief systems. Regardless of educational background and training, every person has a personality that impacts their work style. There was an art in learning people and how to nurture their strengths to get the best performance. Their performance was a mirror of my guidance and coaching. I would always ask myself how can I assign tasks and distribute workloads to match the skill sets of those I intended to develop.

Over some years, it became very apparent that I could not hire and train people to have good character or integrity. These are all attributes innate to the individual. These are God-given qualities that an individual must cherish and desire to foster. However, I could offer honest feedback, affirmations, and opportunities to let them shine.

If most of us were assigned a task to describe a character in a book, television show, or movie, the response would likely come easy. However, describing character is to interpret personality and behavior, which speak to an individual's makeup. It is amazing how quickly opinions and perceptions are formulated of others, simply from one encounter or interaction. Yet, character speaks through all the noise. Character is the definition of who you are and the very essence of your reputation that arrives in the room before you do. Character is the thing you stand on, the foundation of your very being.

Defining your why is the most critical area of self-awareness you will experience. Your why is simply your purpose, who you are, and what you value. I believe these areas of self-awareness act as a mental compass of morality, known as character.

In a professional work environment, the character of its employees contributes to the work culture. Ask yourself, *Is the environment welcoming? Are staff respectful, non-judgmental, and approachable? Do staff exhibit passion for the work? Are staff kind, and do they seek to improve the well-being of others?*

GROW IN INTEGRITY

Integrity—the quality of being honest and having strong moral principles

Truth and consistency say a lot about the quality of work or product being produced. It demonstrates a level of care and concern for the work you do. Anything you value, you take care of with clear intention.

Having been a sworn officer of the court for more than twenty years required me to be mindful of my conduct and involvements on and off the clock. Whether under a watchful eye or not, I had to care about me. It's about self-value and having a God-consciousness. Walking in integrity means understanding you have a purpose and that choices impact your life and often the lives of others around you.

Mean what you say and say what you mean is a way to walk with integrity. Over many years, I have watched members of leadership not address issues head-on or use passive-aggressive approaches to problem solving. These styles of management rarely address the core of the issue and often contribute to staff morale and retention issues. Where there is no vision, a people perish. Those in leadership roles must be clear about expectations and the end goal. Leaders also must be honest with those they lead about their performance and areas needing improvement. I have had the incredible opportunity to contribute to the development of many leaders, and the reward is seeing their successful careers.

Integrity also means being true to oneself and willingness to step into unknown places. Humility goes a long way when treading unfamiliar territory. I had to learn to be okay with acknowledging what I did not know, so the things I knew had the space to shine through. Are you willing to ask for help? Are you willing to seek out mentorship? Are you willing to take risks?

GROW IN GRIT AND GRIND

Grit—courage, resolve and strength, perseverance; ability to maintain focus/work ethic

Grind—hard work, hustle, disciplined approach

When I first entered graduate school, my practicum was a year assignment at a state mental health hospital. Stepping out of my comfort zone was an understatement since this placement was focused on micro-clinical social work, yet my concentration was macro-systems social work. Placement in the opposite track was commonly used as an intentional design of the program. At first, I thought maybe it would be in the forensic unit, yet I was assigned to the medical unit with highly disabled and severely deformed adults.

I was young, totally unprepared, and scared. Some of these adults were non-vocal with limited mobility, missing limbs like eyes, ears, partial noses, and functioning at the cognitive learning levels of small children. Many had no family, no friends, and were totally disconnected from people outside the facility. It was my responsibility to assess needs, enhance communications, and reconnect family where possible.

In full transparency, this experience felt completely uncomfortable and impossible.

Surprisingly, my gifts in arts and music allowed me to exercise extreme creativity to communicate using colors, sounds, lights, toys, et cetera. I eventually coordinated a pet therapy project that worked wonders and milestones. I was also able to reunite some of the patients with family members. The blessing was that God had a purpose and surrounded me with an incredible group of nurses, all heavily involved in ministry in some way. These women of God helped me to function in uncomfortable and unfamiliar territory, growing in courage and perseverance all along the way. This was my first introduction to professional grit and grind.

The second part of my practicum and employment was as a pretrial investigator. It required me to enter the jail by 4:30 a.m. and conduct interviews with individuals to determine bond eligibility. I had interactions with all backgrounds, having close contact in small spaces with only a chair or table in between. Interviews were largely conducted without the presence of a deputy or guard in sight. This exposed me to the raw internal workings of the criminal justice system, which was not business suits, pristine hallways, or courtrooms. My exposure to area jails over many years does not compare to those working behind the wall of maximum-security lockdown facilities. However, the reality and stench of human beings locked behind gates and doors is the same. Many acted just like animals in cages—inappropriate looks, sexual gestures, and foul language.

After investigations, those eligible for release pending trial were placed under supervision. I soon realized many were simply people with complicated situations, products of their environments, and/or systemic societal holds. I witnessed the harsh reality of those struggling with criminal thinking and antisocial personalities, those lacking remorse, and those suffering from abuse and addiction. God was taking me further into the grit and grind.

The definition of humanity was much clearer, and I grew an appreciation for the breath of God moving through my lungs every day. God was again positioning me in uncomfortable, unfamiliar territory. He was showing me new humility and showing me his face.

Once I was promoted to a supervisor, the early part of my journey in management was difficult. I was much younger than the staff I supervised, and I was the first female manager who was a woman of color in the agency's history. Like many counties and cities across the country, women of color were and are considerably disproportionate in leadership positions in comparison to the demographic composition of the county itself.

My immediate management colleagues were all white males who had well-established relationships with stakeholders, such as county leadership, police, prosecutors, and an all-white judiciary. I was not invited to the golf course lunches nor privy to certain conversations. I quickly learned that my work performance would need to speak for me. It was during those early years in my career, I truly learned how to play this game called grit and grind. It required me to look sharper, be smarter, move a step ahead, and be more visible than my counterparts. I was again in unfamiliar territory.

My long-term boss and mentor retired after thirty-plus years in the field. He was an older gentleman, always believing in my abilities and pushing me beyond what I thought I could handle. He was incredibly supportive throughout my career and is still someone I consider a friend to this very day. He taught me the importance of believing people can change, developing those under my leadership, leading with emotional intelligence, and to always present as polished.

Not only was this next uncomfortable season learning about the administrative level of legal political systems and justice, but it took me deeper into the minds and experiences of those who hurt and abuse—those with unimaginable backgrounds of trauma, mental health, and addiction. It exposed me to victims and survivors of violence and abuse in ways too graphic to explain on these pages. I was one of the first members who worked to form the county's domestic violence fatality review team, where I reviewed well over sixty cases of domestic violence homicide suicides over many years. God was transcending me into avenues of spiritual warfare, gifts, and insight way outside of familiar places—dark places that only the light of Jesus could heal. It is amazing how your spiritual gifts have purpose and design in the natural.

Not only was I stepping out spiritually and professionally, but I was also planting seeds. While building, you must have roots that can withstand the grit and the grind process. If well developed and maintained, the roots will continue to give life. Working through grit requires perseverance, and working through grind requires endurance.

GROW IN GRACE

Grace—simple elegance and refinement

Over the last several years, the term *grace* has been used loosely more often in movies and conversations to acknowledge a challenge or when someone is being too hard on themselves or others. It is not uncommon to hear someone say, "Give yourself some grace, give them some grace, or we need to extend more grace." This is simply a way of meeting people where they are, taking the time to listen and understand the position of other perspectives when they differ from your own. Understand that every person hears, experiences, processes, and responds to information differently. Likewise, every person moves at different stages and seasons. No person can operate at one hundred percent all the time. In a professional environment, it is appropriate to expect excellence and quality; however, recognize that flexibility and kindness is essential. Move wisely in every situation and move with grace that reflects patience, elegance, and refinement.

Strong leaders must balance communication style, as they are often misunderstood, judged, and labeled particularly by those closest to them. Communication styles used in professional work environments often do not translate the same way in personal environments. Perceptions of you likely differ between professional colleagues versus close family and friends. Grace should be used and equally given to those around us.

Early in my career as a young manager, my expectations were excessively high for myself and those of my team. As wisdom grew, I did not lower my standard, but I did alter my approach. I learned to extend grace, as opportunities for growth exist in spaces of imperfection.

In closing, this new level of my career meant stepping away from a twenty-year position of comfort, which I knew and performed well.

Stepping out of your comfort zone means stepping into places of a higher calling and responsibility. Every step of my journey was ordered by the Lord. He had already equipped and prepared me. God's grace and unmerited favor never runs out.

TISHA SKINNER

Tisha Skinner has more than twenty-seven years of experience in criminal justice services. She is the local probation coordinator, where she serves as a subject matter expert in evidence-based practices. At the start of her career, she worked as a pretrial investigator and later a probation supervisor where she developed the first specialized local domestic violence probation unit in the state of Virginia. Tisha has extensive managerial experience, including policy and procedure development, employee leadership, professional development, team building, and performance evaluation.

Tisha has extensive experience serving and/or leading a host of local, state, and national workgroups, committees, boards, and organizations designed to improve system response, coordination, and service delivery. Tisha has eighteen years in skill-based curriculum development and also serves as a state trainer for new local pretrial-probation officers, agency directors, and front-line supervisors. She is a certified substance abuse mental health service administration trainer for Trauma Improved Criminal Justice Responses. Tisha has a passion for change management, program development, and building leaders.

Tisha completed her studies through Virginia State University, where she obtained a bachelor of arts in political science and pre-law. She also attended Virginia Commonwealth University, where she completed forty-eight credit hours of extensive coursework and two professional practicums as part of the master of social work program. She received a master's of human services and criminal justice from Capella University.

Tisha is a native of New Jersey and a dedicated mother of two who loves the Lord. She has served in music ministry more than twenty-five years as a praise and worship leader. She has also served in ministry assisting those who have experienced trauma, women, and youth ministry activities.

Other Titles by
Dr. Valarie Harris

www.ingramcontent.com/pod-product-compliance
Lightning Source LLC
Chambersburg PA
CBHW060332130626
46553CB00003B/990